52 Ohio Weekends

GREAT GETAWAYS AND ADVENTURES FOR EVERY SEASON

MARY QUINLEY

COUNTRY ROADS PRESS
NTC/Contemporary Publishing Group

Library of Congress Cataloging-in-Publication Data

Quinley, Mary.
    52 Ohio Weekends / Mary Quinley.
       p.   cm.
    Includes index.
    ISBN 1-56626-184-8 (paper)
    1. Ohio—Guidebooks.   I. Title.
  F489.3.Q56   1997
  917.104'43—dc21   97-10053
                                       CIP

Cover and interior design by Nick Panos
Cover and interior illustrations copyright © Jill Banashek
Map by Mapping Specialists, Madison, Wisconsin
Picture research by Elizabeth Broadrup Lieberman

Published by Country Roads Press
A division of NTC/Contemporary Publishing Group, Inc.
4255 West Touhy Avenue, Lincolnwood (Chicago), Illinois 60712-1975 U.S.A.
Copyright © 1999 by Mary Quinley
Printed in the United States of America
International Standard Book Number: 1-56626-184-8

99 00 01 02 03 04 QP 19 18 17 16 15 14 13 12 11 10 9 8 7 6 5 4 3 2 1

For Fred and Jonathan—
the two special men in my life—
and Dad—
my greatest fan in Heaven

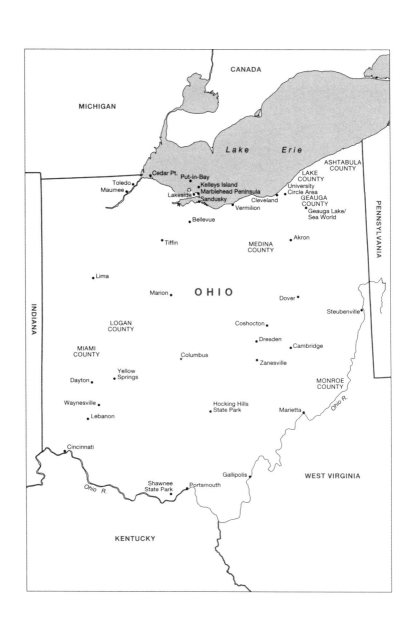

CANADA

MICHIGAN

Lake   Erie

ASHTABULA
COUNTY

Cedar Pt. •Put-in-Bay
Toledo •   • Kelleys Island   LAKE
Maumee •   Marblehead Peninsula COUNTY
          Lakeside • •Sandusky   University
                  • Vermilion   Circle Area
                          Cleveland GEAUGA
                                    COUNTY
                          • Geauga Lake/
          • Bellevue   Sea World

          • Tiffin   MEDINA   • Akron
                          COUNTY

      • Lima

      Marion •   **OHIO**

                          Dover •
                                    Steubenville •

          LOGAN   Coshocton •
          COUNTY

      MIAMI   • Dresden
      COUNTY   • Cambridge
                  Columbus •
          Yellow   • Zanesville
    Dayton • Springs

  Waynesville •   MONROE
                              COUNTY
      • Lebanon   Hocking Hills   *Ohio R.*
                  State Park • Marietta •

PENNSYLVANIA

INDIANA

  • Cincinnati

          Ohio R.   Shawnee   Gallipolis •
                        State Park • Portsmouth   WEST VIRGINIA

      KENTUCKY

Contents

Central

Southeast

Southwest

Introduction

MY EARLIEST MEMORIES OF OHIO INVOLVE FAMILY. MY FATHER would often tell the story about why he was born in Toledo. According to Dad, my Grandmother Diroff "liked a doctor in Toledo." She insisted that Grandpa drive her across the state line, from "whatever Michigan town they were living in," to Toledo, each time her "due date" approached. Grandma and Grandpa made eight "timely" journeys—with one trip resulting in twin births.

I can't comment about the medical profession in Ohio, but I can attest to the fact that the Buckeye State offers great getaway opportunities geared for families, singles, couples, and seniors alike.

One of the easiest ways to make Ohio travel plans is to call the state's tourism hot line: 800-BUCKEYE. Here's the lowdown on this complete travel information line:

- Callers can access information on thousands of Ohio activities and attractions twenty-four hours a day, seven days a week. The service is free of charge.

- Ohio travel planners can be ordered through the automated system any time of the day or night.

- Trained travel counselors are available from 8 A.M. to 9 P.M., Monday through Friday, and from 9 A.M. to 6 P.M. on Saturday and Sunday. These counselors have a database of detailed information on events, attractions, festivals, sites, and accommodations.

- In early autumn, callers can request fall foliage updates by calling the same 800 number.

Another way to access the information is to visit the Division of Travel and Tourism website at www.ohiotourism.com.

52 Ohio Weekends is divided into five sections by geographic region. Ski resorts are found in several regions, with the majority located in the northeast part of the state. For this reason, the chapter on skiing, "Downhill Thrills," is included in the Northeast section of the book.

A special "thanks" to all the gracious people in Ohio who spent time helping me gather information. I couldn't have finished my project without your kind assistance.

Warm hugs to my favorite copilots: Fred, Jonathan, Mom, and Vicki. Thanks for sharing the road trips with me. I'm especially grateful to all my Michigan relatives and my Florida family for their encouragement. And, finally, to "the neighborhood gang," thanks for the "tea" breaks.

Northeast

1

More than Oats

AKRON

Quaker Square

MOM WRINKLES HER NOSE AT THE THOUGHT OF EATING oatmeal. But she didn't object to spending the night in the converted 120-foot-high storage silos built by the Quaker Oats Company in downtown Akron.

Thanks to Ferdinand Schumacher and his 1800s home-made oatmeal, a hotel/dining/shopping complex called Quaker Square evolved on the factory site that once housed more than one million bushels of grain.

Take a stroll along the corridor that connects the circular Hilton Inn and the modest-size shops. You'll probably have to stop along your route and let the kids push the buttons that operate the model train displays. Once you're inside the brick structure, you'll discover specialty stores filled with knickknacks, flavored coffee and tea varieties, kitchen utensils, and apparel. As you browse the narrow hallways that connect the shops, be on the lookout for remains of factory milling equipment that is nicely displayed for visitors.

As your mini shopping spree winds down, there's just one more item you might want to consider. Wander back to the first floor, take a deep breath in, and follow the tempting aroma. You'll soon find yourself in a shop that bakes soft, just-from-the-oven oatmeal cookies. Go ahead, buy a bag "to go." You won't be disappointed.

Akron Zoo

Early settlers to the New World traveled across the ocean, bringing their livestock with them. At the Akron Zoo (five minutes southwest of downtown), a replica of one of the colonial ships that made the journey provides endless entertainment for the younger set. Monkey bars and a slide allow the kids to work off some of their endless energy. At the same time, they're absorbing a lesson in domestic livestock without realizing it.

Each morning before the zoo gates open, staff members bury treasures in the Fossil Dig Site. Little visitors search diligently for pieces of petrified dinosaur bones, shark's teeth, arrowheads, and colorful, polished stones. If you find something, it's yours to take home.

Before leaving the grounds, check out the more than two hundred birds, mammals, and reptiles on exhibit. Then encourage the youngsters to play hide-and-seek in the three-foot-high, make-believe eagle's nest.

Stan Hywet Hall

Hear ye! Hear ye! It must be November. A luscious feast in traditional medieval style, complete with Waldorf salad served in pewter bowls, succulent short ribs, new potatoes, homemade fruitcake, and pitchers of ale, lures holiday guests. You'll want to make your reservations well in advance, as this annual party at Stan Hywet (say: HEE-wit) Hall is extremely popular.

Stan Hywet Hall served as home for forty years to the family of Frank A. Seiberling, cofounder of Goodyear Tire and Rubber Company. The friendly, outgoing spirit of the Seiberling clan continues today. Non Nobis Solum (Not for Us Alone) reads the plaque over the mansion's front entrance, a lasting reminder that guests are always welcome.

The spectacular, spacious rooms and corridors, as well as the colorful and well-groomed gardens, are open to the general public. As you wander through the mansion on a tour, note the detailed carved paneling, the molded plaster ceilings, and the vibrant stained-glass windows.

Can't make it to the Madrigal Dinner? Then, perhaps the family would enjoy a special Christmas tour during the holiday season. Or visit during the summer and watch live performances of Shakespeare's plays in the courtyard near the Carriage House. Stan Hywet Hall is open year-round.

More Akron-Area Attractions

- One option for beginning a weekend jaunt to Quaker Square and the downtown sites is to reserve a seat on the Cuyahoga Valley Scenic Railroad. Passengers are transported twenty-six miles from a train depot in Independence to Akron, dropped off for several hours to shop, dine, or explore the museums, and then returned via the train to Independence. Train schedules vary according to the time of year. Call ahead before making plans.

- The nine galleries of the art deco building at the Kent State University Fashion Museum overflow with a stunning collection of costumes, textiles, glass, porcelains, and paintings. A joint arrangement between the museum and the school provides the general public access to the fabulous displays, while allowing students the opportunity to examine 19th- and 20th-century designer techniques.

- Works by Andy Warhol, Frank Stella, and Helen Frankenthaler contrast with the elegant portraits and impressionist landscapes at the Akron Art Museum. In addition to these permanent collections, temporary exhibits are presented every ten weeks. Admission is free.

- The Goodyear World of Rubber exhibit is located on the fourth floor of Goodyear Hall in downtown Akron. A series of graphic and dimensional displays traces the history of "the Rubber Capital." You can view a simulated rubber plantation, moon-tire display, artificial heart, and Indianapolis 500 race cars. The exhibit is closed Saturdays, Sundays, and holidays. No admission fee.

- Experience life as it was in the mid-1800s at Hale Farm & Village. Watch the blacksmith, glassblower, candle maker, and basket maker skillfully create crafts. A brick maker demonstrates the process used prior to the industrial revolution.

  In 1810, Jonathan Hale left civilized Connecticut and settled in the wilderness of the early Reserve (near present-day Akron). The restored village and working farm areas provide a glimpse of the lifestyle that Hale and his family encountered. Admission fee charged.

- Eat chocolate, see it being made, and purchase a bag "for the road" at Harry London's Chocolate Factory and Hall of Fame. The admission fee includes a chocolate sample, factory tour, and Hall of Fame tour.

Northeast

For More Information

Contact the Akron/Summit Convention & Visitors Bureau, 77 East Mill Street, Akron, OH 44308; 800-245-4254 or 330-374-7560. Website: www.visitakron-summit.org.

Other contacts: Akron Hilton Inn, 135 South Broadway, Akron, OH 44308; 330-253-5970. The Akron Zoo, 500 Edgewood Avenue, Akron, OH 44307; 330-375-2550. Stan Hywet Hall and Gardens, 714 North Portage Path, Akron, OH 44303-1399; 330-836-5533. Cuyahoga Valley Scenic Railroad, 1630 West Mill, Peninsula, OH 44264; 800-468-4070. Kent State University Fashion Museum, PO Box 5190, Kent, OH 44242-0001; 330-672-3450. Akron Art Museum, 70 East Market Street, Akron, OH 44308-2084; 330-376-9185. Goodyear World of Rubber, 1144 East Market Street, Akron, OH 44316; 330-796-2121. Hale Farm & Village, 2686 Oak Hill Road, PO Box 296, Bath, OH 44210-0296; 800-589-9703 or 330-666-3711. Harry London's Chocolate Factory and Hall of Fame, 5353 Lauby Road, North Canton, OH 44720; 800-321-0444.

More than Oats

2

Rockin' on the North Coast

CLEVELAND

IT'S ONLY ROCK AND ROLL, BUT YOU'LL *LOVE* IT!

High-tech wizardry, innovative films and videos, and an impressive gallery of musical "greats" pack the rooms at the Rock and Roll Hall of Fame and Museum in Cleveland. The extensive collection of personal memorabilia includes Buddy Holly's high-school diploma; a leather stage outfit and guitar that belonged to Elvis Presley; and Keith Moon's report card ("shows promise in music").

Not a rock fan? Then, perhaps the museum's rhythm and blues, soul, country, or folk music exhibits will be more appealing.

Entrance to the museum is by timed admission. Tickets may be purchased in advance by calling 800-493-ROLL (493-7655) or by contacting any TicketMaster outlet. The museum is located in Cleveland's North Coast Harbor district.

Cleveland's to-do list extends beyond rock and roll. You'll need at least a handful of weekend trips to get a sense of the thriving metropolis that parallels Lake Erie. Here's a sampling of the town's top attractions:

More North Coast Harbor

- Tour Lake Erie and the Cuyahoga (an Indian word meaning "crooked river") aboard the impressive *Goodtime III*, a sight-seeing and entertainment cruise ship. The one-thousand-passenger, triple-deck ship delights riders with laid-back, relaxing cruises from May through October.

- A golfer's paradise! Ohio ranks sixth in the nation for number of golfing facilities, and more than half of the state's courses are located in the Greater Cleveland area. The courses vary from a sporting par-three to championship layouts.

- Friends and families gather at The Great Lakes Science Center, one of Cleveland's newest additions, for an afternoon adventure. More than 350 interactive exhibits earn the museum the distinct ranking of "the ninth-largest hands-on science museum in the United States." The center's six-story Omnimax Theater features the largest projection system in the world. Viewers are seated at a slight recline while they watch a movie on a dome-like screen.

- The steamship *William G. Mather* hauled iron ore and coal to Cleveland's steel plants for more than a half century. Today it's a floating museum open to the public from May through October. As you wander throughout the ship, pay particular attention to the elaborate, oak-paneled and brass-appointed Pilot House.

The Flats

- Summertime in Cleveland—and the living is easy. Converted warehouses furnish a potpourri of eateries, nightclubs, and breweries in The Flats, an area of flatland on both banks of the Cuyahoga River. Restaurant patio chairs fill quickly. Extra-wide umbrellas shield the lunch crowd from the high-noon heat. A freighter slips by—moving at a steady, slow pace.

This tranquil scene is in sharp contrast to the city's atmosphere approximately 150 years ago. During the mid-1830s, the west side of the river was called Ohio City and the east side was named Cleveland. War erupted between the two rivalries. Finally, in 1854 a peaceful settlement was reached when Ohio City became a part of Cleveland.

- For a soothing pause from your hectic schedule, book a ride (April through October) on the *Nautica Queen*, a 400-passenger luxury cruise-and-dining ship. Lake Erie and Cuyahoga River cruises are offered daily.

Why Cleveland?
General Moses Cleaveland founded the city of Cleveland (spelled Cleaveland) in 1796. On January 6, 1831, the first issue of the *Cleveland Advertiser*, a weekly Whig newspaper, appeared without the "a." The reason? The editor wanted to fit the city's name on a newspaper masthead.

Ohio City

Once I was inside the West Side Market, I really wanted to watch the young man with the saw do what he does best—cut meat. However, when he informed me that it was a lamb, I mumbled, "Thank you" and wandered over to a neighboring display of shiny apples and plump, purple grapes. It's true that West Side Market has a reputation for fresh meats, as well as fish, vegetables, fruits, baked goods, cheeses, and lots more.

Customers arrive at the indoor/outdoor (weather permitting) mammoth marketplace in search of homemade pierogi, no-salt peanut butter, eight-inch pecan rolls, Indian spices, barbecued ribs, and fruit pies. As they shop, they are surrounded by a blend of tantalizing aromas.

The Old World–style market, built in 1912, provides space for more than one hundred merchants who represent a multitude of ethnic groups. Hours of operation vary according to the day. Closed on Sundays.

The Zoo

The Cleveland Metroparks Zoo, one of the country's oldest zoos, is located just five miles south of downtown. In addition to housing "traditional" animals and displays, this complex features a spectacular two-story exhibit dubbed the RainForest. Wander throughout the tropical wilderness. There is so much to observe here! Watch for the giant anteater, the sloth, and dozens of tropical birds. You'll learn why frogs and toads are vulnerable to pollutants. Experience the power of a tropical rainstorm—without getting wet.

Don't be surprised if the afternoon begins to slip away and you're still enthralled with the RainForest. Not to worry—return tomorrow and explore the rest of the zoo!

A Shopper's Paradise

Did you know that the country's first enclosed shopping center was built in downtown Cleveland? Three levels of specialty stores and boutiques are enclosed in the Arcade, an atrium-style mall dating back to 1890.

- Terminal Tower, a renovated train depot, houses an upscale shopping mecca known as the Avenue. Located at Tower City Center, the Avenue sports more than one hundred shops, eateries, and entertainment facilities.

- Save energy for some other downtown shopping in the Prospect-Gateway area and the Warehouse District. In addition to shops, the historic Warehouse District boasts some impressive architectural buildings dating from 1850 through 1920, eclectic art galleries, and diverse dining possibilities.

For More Information

Information on all of the attractions mentioned here can be obtained by contacting the Convention & Visitors Bureau of Greater Cleveland, 3100 Terminal Tower, 50 Public Square, Cleveland, OH 44113; 800-321-1001 or 216-621-5555. Website: www.travelcleveland.com.

Other contacts: Rock and Roll Hall of Fame and Museum, One Key Plaza, Cleveland, OH 44114-1022; 800-493-ROLL or 216-781-ROCK (781-7635). *Goodtime III*, 825 East Ninth Street Pier, Cleveland, OH 44114; 216-861-5110. The Great Lakes Science Center, 601 Erieside Avenue, Cleveland, OH 44114; 216-694-2020. Steamship *William G. Mather*, 1001 East Ninth Street Pier, Cleveland, OH 44114; 216-574-6262. The Flats Oxbow Association, 1283 Riverbed Street, Cleveland, OH 44113; 216-566-1046. *Nautica Queen*, 1153 Main Avenue, Cleveland, OH 44115; 216-696-8888. West Side Market, West 25th Street and Lorain Avenue, Cleveland, OH 44113; 216-664-3386. Cleveland Metroparks Zoo & Rain-Forest, 3900 Brookside Park Drive, Cleveland, OH 44109; 216-661-6500.

13

Rockin' on the North Coast

3

Canal Country

COSHOCTON

IF YOU SPEND ENOUGH TIME IN OHIO, CHANCES ARE YOU'LL hear about the canal era. One stretch of the canals, which opened up isolated rivers in the state, ran from Cleveland on Lake Erie in the north, to Portsmouth on the Ohio River in the south. Cheap transportation for people and goods resulted in an economic boom for many of the towns along the route.

Coshocton County, a spectacular blend of the Appalachian foothills coupled with the valley of three rivers (Walhonding, Tuscarawas, and Muskingum) that converge, reaped the benefits of canal traffic. Today the county delivers multiple options for a family outing.

For starters, plan an afternoon at Roscoe Village, a restored Ohio & Erie Canal community, located in the town of Coshocton.

Before you explore the village's historic buildings, stop at the visitor center for a great overview of the canal system. Miniature dioramas, working locks, an aqueduct model, and a theater production provide insight to the once-thriving shipping port.

Take the youngsters by the hand and stroll outdoors. You'll discover a 19th-century village laced with brick sidewalks and pocket gardens. Wander inside the print shop. Who wants to take a turn pulling the handle on the hand-operated printing press? The 1840s printing machine is one of several village hands-on activities.

"We let the children weave using a two-hundred-year-old loom," said Wilma Hunt, historian of Roscoe Village. "They press on the pedal and pull a bar. They each get a chance. They love it!"

Continue your trek through the restored community. Watch the blacksmith; see a cooper make buckets; marvel at the pottery maker using an old-fashioned kick wheel.

In 1979, the Johnson-Humrickhouse Museum opened at Roscoe Village. Spend some time perusing this memorial planned by John and David Johnson, two Coshocton-born brothers, who were world travelers and who dedicated their impressive collection to their parents. The museum's rooms are adorned with Native American artifacts, an Americana assortment of antique firearms, vintage currency and coin, and authentic period clothing.

After visiting the museum, head for the shops.

"We have a lot of specialty shops—a basket shop, a general store, candy, music, and old-fashioned hardware stores. We also have village-made crafts—pottery, wooden toys, wooden buckets, and brooms. You can buy the same items that you see being made on your tour of the village," said Jan McKenna, director of marketing and education at Roscoe Village.

When you've finished the mini shopping trip, Jan recommends a leisurely walk (or drive) to the canal boat dock, a distance of just less than a mile.

She explained, "The canal boat is not part of the village. However, if you walk from the village to the canal boat, you will be walking either next to the lock or in the lock, now filled with grass, and then across the bridge."

Once you've reached the dock area, book a ride on the *Monticello III*, a horse-drawn canal boat. Are you ready for a nostalgic journey that moves at a snail's pace? The flattop boat glides through a restored section of the canal at a top speed of 3 mph. The forty-five-minute trip along the Walhonding (a Delaware Indian word meaning "white woman") River is a great ending to your canal-themed adventure.

More in Coshocton County

- Sip, sample, and tour. Rainbow Hills Vineyards, a year-round winery in the eastern hills of the county, offers a variety of dinner and dessert wines with intriguing labels, including Trillium, Drumming Grouse, and Prism. When the weather gets warmer, bring the gang to a Summer Steak Fry. From late autumn to early spring, the winery hosts five-course dinners. Call and make a reservation.

- If you arrive before noon, odds are good that the cheese-making process will be in full swing at the Pearl Valley Cheese shop in the town of Fresno. Three generations of the Stalder family have carried on the tradition of cheese making. There are no scheduled tours of the operation, but they welcome you to look around.

- Interested in pottery? Then, visit the Three Rivers Pottery factory in Coshocton. Be there in the morning and you'll see the potters at work. You'll also find an outlet where you can purchase pottery.

- Four blocks from the center of Coshocton there's Royce Craft Baskets, a small, family-run business. Travelers are welcome to come in and watch the basket-making process, or visit the basket outlet which is located at Roscoe Village.

Canal Country

For More Information

For information on the village attractions, contact Roscoe Village, 381 Hill Street, Coshocton, OH 43812; 800-877-1830 or 740-622-9310. The *Monticello III* canal boat is operated seasonally by the Coshocton Park District, 23253 State Route 83, Coshocton, OH 43812; 740-622-7528. The park also operates the Lake Park Recreation Area which includes: Hilltop Golf Course, camping facilities, swimming, and horseback riding. During the winter, ice-skating and cross-country skiing are popular outdoor sports.

Other area contacts: Rainbow Hills Vineyards, 26349 Township Road 251, Newcomerstown, OH 43832; 740-545-9305. Pearl Valley Cheese, 54760 Township Road 90, Fresno, OH 43824; 740-545-6002. Three Rivers Pottery, 1435 South Sixth Street, Coshocton, OH 43812; 740-622-4154. Royce Craft Baskets, PO Box 144, Coshocton, OH 43812; 800-882-1128.

For information on all attractions in Coshocton County, contact the Coshocton County Convention & Visitors Bureau, PO Box 905, Coshocton, OH 43812; 800-338-4724.

Northeast

4

"Mooney's" Museum

DOVER

During the summer of 1913, Ernest "Mooney" Warther was a very busy man. The wood-carver, who lived in the town of Dover, created an unusual-shaped carving and called it his "pliers tree."

"There were no shavings or dust when Dad finished the tree," said David Warther, Ernest's son, who is also a wood-carver.

The tree, made up of more than 500 pairs of miniature pliers, was carved from a solid block of walnut. The slim piece of walnut measured two inches high, two and a half inches wide, and thirteen inches long. When Warther completed the carving, the block of wood magically transformed into his "pliers tree."

David further explains: "It looks like a tree. The trunk is the first pair of pliers, and the branches are individual pliers."

Today, comfortably settled in the rolling Tuscarawas Valley, dubbed "The Little Switzerland of Ohio," Warther's family displays his "pliers tree" and more of his one-of-a-kind carvings at the Warther Museum in Dover.

Several museums, a winery, a cheese house, and a side trip to the neighboring town of Sugarcreek supply the basic ingredients for a relaxed getaway excursion.

Pocket-size wooden pliers were a Warther specialty. He carved more than 750,000 pairs and used them as a symbol of family unity. During the Great Depression, the pliers sold for a nickel. If Warther failed to finish the carving within twenty seconds, the customer got the pliers free of charge.

As you amble through the rooms on your guided tour of the museum, you'll learn that master-carver Warther admired Abraham Lincoln. One of the "favorites" with museumgoers is the eight-foot-long replica of Lincoln's funeral train, created by Warther in dollhouse proportions. Be sure to peek through the tiny lit windows of the train. The beautifully carved draperies, an eagle insignia, and the coffin were made of ebony, ivory, and pearl to commemorate the centennial anniversary of Lincoln's death.

There's so much more to marvel at: a model walnut-and-ivory 18th-century steel mill where Warther worked (check out the petite foreman who is obviously upset with the sleeping worker, and see if you can find the miniature figure that represents Ernest himself); intricately carved Civil War memorabilia; and ebony, ivory, and walnut models of steam engines dating back to 250 B.C.

One of the most impressive engines in the collection, the DeWitt Clinton, was named for a 19th-century governor of New York. It has maintained a steady pace of continuous motion for more than eighty years because Warther used arguto, an oily wood found in South America that provides a natural lubricant.

How did Warther, a second-grade dropout with no formal education, create such authentic carvings?

"My grandfather thought carving was a God-given talent. However, he believed that carving came after people—he always had time to talk to the kids," said Carol (Warther) Moreland, granddaughter of Ernest.

If you visit the museum on weekdays, be sure to wander by the knife carvers' shop to catch a glimpse of the skilled workers in action. Making knives was another Warther talent; he sold kitchen cutlery to supplement his income.

Before you leave the grounds, stroll outdoors to the brick building adjacent to the museum. Warther saved enough nickels from his pliers' sales to build this one-room structure for his wife, Freida. She was a button collector. The walls and ceiling are smothered with more than 72,000 buttons, all neatly displayed in a variety of star-, swirl-, diamond-, and circle-shape designs.

Once you've finished admiring the Warther family's hobbies, if the weather is cooperating, mosey through the flower gardens and head for the picnic area. Sit for a spell and consider your options for the next leg of your journey.

More Dover Area Sites

- If 19th-century ornate chandeliers, fine china, and period furniture interest you, plan to take a guided tour of the J. E. Reeves Victorian Home and Museum on Iron Avenue. This turn-of-the-century farmhouse, remodeled to reflect the standards of a Dover industrialist, features hundreds of antiques that belonged to the Reeves family. Visitors are encouraged to linger in the mansion's elegant rooms, none having roped-off areas.

- After your museum tours, venture west a few miles to the outskirts of town. You'll be driving on State Route 39, through an Amish-populated landscape dotted with gentle curves and patchwork hills. Watch for the barn with the larger-than-life, plump grapes painted on its side. You've reached DerMarktplatz, affectionately labeled the "purple place." It houses a gift shop, deli, and wine cellar. Wander inside for some samples of smoked German meats and an assortment of cheeses. You'll find shelves of handmade Amish quilts, a variety of cookbooks, and gourmet foods. In the back room the "over twenty-one" crowd are invited to sip Cabernet sauvignon, spiced apple, and dandelion wines.

"We make the largest variety of fruit and berry wines in the country," said Dalton Bixler, owner and wine maker. "We average at least ten at all times."

- Just a stone's throw away from DerMarktplatz, on the opposite side of the bend in the road, sits the Broad Run Cheesehouse. Take a tour of the cheese factory. You'll receive a souvenir sailor-type hat and samples of cheeses. If you happen to be looking for ruffled country curtains or fancy Victorian wares, browse through the gift shop before leaving the Cheesehouse.

- Continue your low-key getaway to the west. Within minutes you'll reach Sugarcreek, a simple community where horse-pulled buggies driven by Amish families are a common sight. Park your car near the main intersection in town, and start walking. A potpourri of pleasing scents seeps from the town's bakery where fresh-from-the-oven goodies fill the shelves. You'll also discover a handful of narrow-front stores that entice browsers to shop for music boxes, Amish dolls, and imports from Switzerland, Austria, and Germany. Hungry? Not a problem. Swiss and Amish-style restaurants serve generous portions of homemade food.

While in Sugarcreek, join the train buffs at the Dennison Railroad Depot Museum. Check the schedule for departures of special train excursions.

For More Information

Warther Museum is open year-round. Call 330-343-7513 or write to Warther Museum, 331 Karl Avenue, Dover, OH 44622, for further information. Dover is located approximately seventy-five miles south of Cleveland.

Other contacts: J. E. Reeves Victorian Home and Museum, Dover Historical Society, 325 East Iron Avenue, Dover, OH 44622; 800-815-2794 or 330-343-7040. DerMarktplatz, 5934 Old State Route 39, Dover, OH 44622; 800-THE-WINE (843-9463) or 330-343-3603. Broad Run Cheesehouse, 6011 Old State Route 39, Box 299, Dover, OH 44622; 800-332-3358 or 330-343-4108. The Reeves Home is open during the summer months and Christmas season; off-season hours are by appointment. Both DerMarktplatz and Broad Run Cheesehouse are open year-round.

Sugarcreek hosts the Ohio Swiss Festival (held the fourth weekend after Labor Day). For information on the festival and Sugarcreek attractions, contact the Alpine Hills Museum, 106 West Main Street, Sugarcreek, OH 44681; 330-852-4113. For information on special train excursions, call 740-922-6776.

For further information on attractions, area restaurants, shopping, and lodging accommodations, contact the Tuscarawas County Convention and Visitors Bureau, 125 McDonald Drive Southwest, New Philadelphia, OH 44663; 800-527-3387 or 330-339-5453. Website: www.neohiotravel.com.

Note: Some attractions, shops, and restaurants are closed on Sundays.

'Mooney's Museum

5

Love That Maple Syrup

GEAUGA COUNTY

Chardon

SOMETIME IN APRIL, DEPENDING ON MOTHER NATURE'S cooperation, the townsfolk in Chardon begin preparations for an annual maple syrup celebration.

"Every day, twice a day, a tractor pulls a stainless-steel tub on a wagon. Buckets of syrup from all the trees around the square and in front of private homes are emptied," said Lynda Chambers, a representative for the Geauga County Tourism Council. Home owners who don't want their trees tapped "put a ribbon or a rope on the tree."

The annual Geauga County Maple Festival, held on Chardon Square, entertains the crowds with lively parades, handmade crafts, primitive arts, educational and historical displays, bathtub races, and Sap Run Marathons. Naturally, maple syrup, maple candy, and pancakes are part of the package.

Chardon's popularity extends beyond syrup and springtime. For instance, during balmy, summer Friday evenings, Chardon Square swings to the tunes of brass bands.

"People gather by the hundreds near the gazebo; they bring picnic baskets, lawn chairs, and blankets," added Chambers.

A year-round craft mall specializing in collectibles, decorations, and wearable arts, and an adventure park with wet and dry activities add to Chardon's family-style charm.

Burton

At the intersection of State Route 87 and State Route 700 (ten miles south of Chardon), cars loop around a small park that is right smack in the middle of a town and features the Burton Log Cabin. In 1931, the cabin was constructed on this central plot of land with the purpose of manufacturing maple-sugar products. Since that time, high-quality light and dark syrup, maple-sugar candy, and maple-cream candy continue to entice customers to visit Burton's log structure.

The cabin's kitchen produces maple syrup in late February and early March; candy is made at least twice a week. If you're an early bird, stop by at 7 A.M. and watch the candy makers at work. When production is at a standstill, watch the video that explains the candy-making process.

Wondering what to do with the pint of pure maple syrup you bought (besides dripping it generously over pancakes and waffles)? Ask the staff for some recipes before you leave the cabin.

Wander across the street from the park to Century Village. This historical complex comprises twenty-one restored buildings filled with artifacts and remnants of 19th-century lifestyles in the Western Reserve. As you walk the grounds, be sure to check out the 1872 schoolhouse and the circa-1798 log cabin. Of particular interest in the Hickox Brick building is an awesome display of more than seven thousand lead miniatures dressed in authentic-detailed uniforms. They depict famous armies dating from ancient Egypt through World War II. This exhibit ranks as "the largest lead miniature collection in the United States."

Tours of Century Village are seasonal.

If you're in the mood for an old-fashioned fair, visit Burton during the Greater Geauga County Fair.

"We try to keep the fair more rural, so it is like the traditional county fairs. There are competitions for canning and needlepoint. There are farm animals, wonderful antiques, and vegetables and fruits. Our biggest attractions are the tractor pulls and the smash-car derby. We now have an all-women's event in the derby," said Chambers.

Family-style entertainment is presented, rather than appearances by big-name stars. The event is always held Labor Day weekend. In 1997, the county celebrated its 174th fair—proud of the fact that Burton is host to the oldest fair in Ohio.

Middlefield

Save an afternoon and explore Middlefield, a neighboring community, claiming to have the second-largest Amish settlement in Ohio.

"The Amish are known for making everything from scratch. Yoder's (a restaurant) serves homemade food, more like what you get in your own kitchen," said Chambers.

She suggests that visitors who want to get a feel for Amish lifestyles should "walk around the town and visit the stores where the Amish buy their clothing and tools."

While in Middlefield, tour the Middlefield Cheese shop. The staff serves samples of its specialty products. After you've tasted some of the cheeses, head outside. Around the corner from the cheese factory, you'll discover (just follow your nose) a bakery stocked with shelves of fresh-from-the-oven goodies. Visit early in the day for best selections.

Love That Maple Syrup

Next door to the bakery is an antiques shop featuring furniture, glassware, postcards, and vintage clothing.

There's another option for a mini shopping jaunt before departing Middlefield: drive a short distance to Settler's Farm. This five-shop village offers an intriguing selection of gifts, collectibles, quilting supplies, and casual clothing.

For More Information

Due to the large Amish population in the county, many of the area businesses are closed on Sunday. Call the establishment before making your plans. Remember to be aware of slow-moving buggies and farm machinery while you are driving in Amish country.

For information on all Geauga County attractions and events, contact the Geauga County Tourism Council, PO Box 556, Chardon, OH 44024; 800-775-TOUR (775-8687). For Burton-area information, contact the Burton Chamber of Commerce, PO Box 537, Burton, OH 44021-0537; 440-834-4204.

6

Masters of Invention

THE ELEMENTARY-AGE YOUNGSTER SITTING AT THE COMPUTER worked diligently at perfecting the lines and curves on the screen.

"What are you drawing?" asked his friend.

"My dad's face!" beamed the aspiring artist.

A sense of humor (sure hope Dad has one) and lots of imagination are all that's needed at Inventure Place, home of the National Inventors Hall of Fame in Akron.

The Inventors Workshop on the bottom level of the museum overflows with hands-on computer-animation exhibits, creation stations, and building utensils for kids of all ages. The spacious floor plan leaves lots of elbow room for inquisitive minds and working hands.

"We give people the tools and environment to create and come up with new ideas. There are no rules," said Stephen Brand, executive director.

A frequent question asked by adult visitors is: "What's here for kids?"

And the answer is: "Plenty." You can do "everything your mom never let you do, as long as no one gets hurt."

For starters, there's the popular station called the Ball Construction Set. It consists of bendable plastic tubes, PVC pipes, and metal rods. Gravity becomes the obstacle as participants work together to build a structure of unlimited configuration possibilities. Kids have been known to linger at this station for hours at a stretch, wander off and try something different, and then return to the Construction Set.

OK, raise your hand if you've ever played a harp—without strings? It doesn't sound plausible. Yet, here at the museum it can be done. As you move your hands, pretending to play the stringless harp, you break the laser beams with the movement—and, miraculously, musical sounds emanate from the instrument. Body movements also trigger the infrared beam at the Body Music Display. With a little practice, the group just might be able to produce a familiar melody. Perhaps someone will create the latest "hit."

Or, you might want to get wet at the water exhibit. Watch out, Mom and Dad! A stream of water squirts eight feet above the ground, with kids controlling the flow by use of laser beams.

If moviemaking interests the gang, check out the video-animation exhibits. Two cameras and a table of props (piles of mock, miniature-size people and animals, different-shaped blocks, and dominoes) provide the tools for motion-picture producing.

Next, go find the "Make it!" station. What a mess! If you plan to stay and work here, put on the required goggles. A three-foot robot stands erect on one of the crowded work-tables. His (or is it her?) body parts include paper cups, insulation, a white telephone cord, and lots of small pieces from the innards of an out-of-date computer. Further perusal reveals a stack of alphabet keys and ribbons from a defunct typewriter.

The museum depends on thousands of used and donated items received from individuals and corporations. Bins stuffed with rubber hoses, clocks, used wire, VCRs, and stereos present endless opportunities for young minds.

Did you know that patents are available for living things, not just machines? Mosey on over to the herb garden and read about the relationship between botany and invention.

Breathe in deeply. Pleasant whiffs of thyme, peppermint, and sweet basil permeate the air.

You'll probably need a short break before you explore the upstairs floors. There's a homey space filled with comfy chairs and a collection of magazines and books relating to inventions and creativity. This area also serves as a great "waiting room" for both parents and kids.

The museum has five tiers dedicated to the men and women inventors of the United States. Exhibits, displays, short biographies, and photographs line the walls. As you meander through the halls, look for an early hand plow invented by John Deere, the extensive scissors display case, and the exhibit that describes the steps of the patent process.

Thomas Edison was the first to be admitted to the National Inventors Hall of Fame. Thus far, more than 120 inventors share space in the museum. Each year a selection committee comprising representatives from national scientific and technical organizations nominates new members. The fifth floor pays tribute to these new inductees.

Remember the young artist at the computer? Perhaps someday he'll earn space on the top floor.

FOR MORE INFORMATION

Inventure Place is open seven days a week. For more details, contact Inventure Place, Home of the National Inventors Hall of Fame, 221 South Broadway, Akron, OH 44308; 800-968-IDEA (968-4332) or 330-762-4463. Website: www.invent.org.

For information on other attractions in the Akron area, contact the Akron/Summit Convention & Visitors Bureau, 77 East Mill Street, Akron, OH 44308; 800-245-4254 or 330-374-7560. Website: www.visitakron-summit.org.

Masters of Invention

7

Double Your Pleasure

LAKE AND ASHTABULA COUNTIES

TWO SIDE-BY-SIDE COUNTIES, LAKE AND ASHTABULA, ARE neatly tucked into Ohio's northeastern corner. Lake Farmpark, situated in Lake County, is only one excuse for planning a journey to the communities hugging the shores of Lake Erie.

Let's take a trek through the region, a scenic thirty- to sixty-minute drive heading eastward from Cleveland, and uncover some of the sites that frequently lure city dwellers and vacationers.

Lake Farmpark

Predawn risers are rare in my crowd. So, when the bus delivered our groggy group to the front entrance of Lake Farmpark at an early hour, there were some skeptics among us.

After perusing the visitor center, we were gently ushered into the dairy parlor. Sitting on bleachers facing a slightly raised platform, we listened to our guide as he shared tidbits about dairy cows and the milking process.

"Anyone ever milk a cow?"

All hands remained down—this audience didn't have a clue about farm chores.

"It's really very easy. Any volunteers? I need some help milking Echo."

"Why not," I mumbled under my breath.

Within seconds, several hands meekly went up (mine included). We then took turns sitting on the short-legged stool and milked Echo, a Brown Swiss dairy cow, who proved to be mild-mannered and very cooperative. No spilled milk here!

In addition to milking cows, city folk get a chance to perform some pretty neat chores when they visit the mammoth grounds of Lake Farmpark. In the spring, visitors help plant potatoes; in the fall, they are invited to harvest the crop. They also get to press apples to make cider.

We finally bid adieu to Echo and her fellow dairy friends and moved outside where a horse-drawn wagon stood ready and waiting to take us exploring. We climbed aboard, balancing cups of fresh coffee and a yummy breakfast croissant baked by the park's kitchen staff.

A dull mist lingered over the farm as our wagon thumped along the country path. Barnyard animals roamed the fields oblivious to our morning intrusion. Lake Farmpark maintains more than fifty breeds of horses, cattle, sheep, goats, swine, and poultry. Many are rare and endangered.

We stopped to watch Queen, a sheepdog, demonstrate her special talent for herding. Then we wandered to the nearby Sheep Show, where we learned that there are eight breeds of sheep living on this farm.

We climbed back into the wagon and continued at a leisurely pace until we reached the Plant Science Center. Our mission, once we were indoors, was to get a close-up view of the Great Tomato Works exhibit, a whimsical, larger-than-life model of a tomato.

The exhibit is impressive.

Try to imagine a tomato seven feet across, with a vine ten inches thick and more than one hundred feet in length.

Once inside the replicated plant you'll discover buttons to push, balls to throw, and cranks to turn. In a very nontraditional method, this exhibit provides unique tools for learning about the life processes of plant growth and food production. What an awesome way to explain pollination, photosynthesis, and the internal plumbing systems of plants.

It was once again time to move on. The morning slipped away as our wagon circled back to the visitor center. Before we climbed back into the bus, a handful of us did a last-minute search in the gift shop for homemade jams and country-style cookbooks. There wasn't a disappointed soul in the group as we headed back to the highway.

More Fun Stuff to Do in Lake County

- Some folks enjoy an occasional game of golf—others *live* to golf. The Quail Hollow Resort & Country Club hosts championship golfers, as well as amateur players, at its lush, hardwood forest course in Concord. Indoor and outdoor pools, a health spa, tennis courts, cross-country groomed trails, and a variety of dining facilities attract year-round patrons.

- Everyone needs an occasional escape from daily stressors. The pathways of the Holden Arboretum, located in the town of Kirtland, provide a perfect setting for private reflection. Flourishing plant life, weathered oak trees (some dating back more than two hundred years), meandering streams, and endless gardens furnish the backdrop for a soothing back-to-nature encounter.

  Take your pick: short walks, rugged hikes, or guided tours. Directional signs, maps, audio guides, and well-marked trails provide easy accessibility to this spectacular natural wonderland.

Double Your Pleasure

- The Kirtland Temple, located in the village of Kirtland, is a distinctive-looking building done in Greek, Georgian, and Gothic architectural styles. The followers of Joseph Smith, Jr., founder of the Latter-day Saint movement, worshiped here in the 1830s. The temple is open to the public, and free tours are offered.

Ashtabula County

- There is something wonderfully refreshing about an afternoon drive through the looping hills and rolling vineyards of Lake Erie's southern shores. Wine produced in this region consistently receives awards for its excellent quality.

  Spend an afternoon discovering the individual charm each of the wineries has to offer. Wine tastings, casual dining, tours, and delightful boutiques add to the relaxed ambiance of the wineries. It's OK to take the kids—many of the wineries produce grape juice and alcohol-free wine.

- Ashtabula represents a mix of city bustle and small-town charisma. Shoppers should be sure to check out the short stretch of shops on Main Avenue. You'll find antiques, crafts, nautical gifts, and handmade apparel.

- Make your way up to the scenic bluff overlooking Ashtabula Harbor for a bird's-eye view of the city. While you're up there, take time to visit two of Ashtabula's museums: the Hubbard House, once used as a northern terminus of the Underground Railroad for escaping slaves, and the Great Lakes Marine & U.S. Coast Guard Museum, a collection of exhibits and artifacts that help preserve the maritime history of the Great Lakes.

- Do antique strollers and old-fashioned toys interest you? If so, you'll want to examine the extensive collections at the Victorian Perambulator Museum in the town of Jefferson. Baby carriages, a train set, dolls, and strollers from bygone days fill the rooms of the privately owned display.

- While in Jefferson, stop and visit the restored historic Lake Shore and Michigan Southern Railroad Station, more frequently called the Jefferson Depot. An original potbelly stove, operational wall-hung flush tanks, and the exclusive "ladies waiting room" are reminiscent of 19th-century lifestyles.

- Ashtabula County boasts to be "the Covered Bridge Capital of Ohio." Take a driving tour any day of the week and you'll understand why this is so. During the second full weekend in October, the county pays tribute to its two dozen bridges at the Covered Bridge Festival. You'll be treated to entertainment, food, and lots of opportunities to explore the nostalgic structures.

- Ashtabula's shoreline is a water lover's haven for anglers, boaters, swimmers, and water-skiers. However, Lake Erie isn't the only water playground in the area. Ashtabula County, with its Pennsylvania neighbor, shares Pymatuning Lake, the largest man-made lake in the eastern part of the United States.

Two counties, tons of fun! So, what are you waiting for?

Double Your Pleasure

For More Information

For information on Lake County attractions, contact the Lake County Visitors Bureau, 1610 Mentor Avenue, Suite 2, Painesville, OH 44077; 800-368-LAKE (368-5253) or 440-

354-2424. Website: www.lakevisit.com. Lake Farmpark, 8800 Chardon Road, Kirtland, OH 44094; 800-366-FARM (366-3276) or 440-256-2122. Quail Hollow, 11080 Concord-Hambden Road, Concord, OH 44077; 800-792-0258. The Holden Arboretum, 9500 Sperry Road, Kirtland, OH 44094; 440-946-4400. Kirtland Temple Historic Center, 9020 Chillicothe Road, Kirtland, OH 44094; 440-256-3318.

For information on Ashtabula County attractions, contact the Ashtabula County Convention & Visitors Bureau, 1850 Austinburg Road, Austinburg, OH 44010; 800-3-DROPIN (337-6746) or 440-275-3202. Website: www.accvb.org.

Other contacts: Ohio Wine Producers Association, PO Box 157, Austinburg, OH 44010; 800-227-6972. Hubbard House, PO Box 2855, Ashtabula, OH 44005; 440-964-8168. Great Lakes Marine & U.S. Coast Guard Museum, 1071-73 Walnut Boulevard, Ashtabula, OH 44004; 440-964-6847. Victorian Perambulator Museum, 26 East Cedar Street, Jefferson, OH 44047; 440-576-9588. Jefferson Depot, 147 East Jefferson Street, Jefferson, OH 44047; 440-293-5532. Covered Bridge Festival, Ashtabula County Covered Bridge Festival Office, 25 West Jefferson Street, Jefferson, OH 44047; 440-576-3769.

Northeast

8

A President's Tribute

THE MCKINLEY

Discover World

ALICE, THE LIFE-SIZE MECHANICAL ALLOSAURUS, GREETS US. She opens her wide jaws ever so slowly and growls. Not to worry. She is just saying, "hello."

We are indoors at Discover World, a museum situated atop a neatly manicured landscape on the highest point in Canton. Discover World is one of three family-style attractions at the McKinley complex.

After admiring Alice, visitors are encouraged to take a seat at the computer around the corner and select a short movie. Features include dinosaur nesting, predation, and extinction. Or pick a geology-related theme and watch the screen as earthquakes and volcanoes form.

As you wander into the gem-and-mineral display section, try to figure out how your mother's pancakes are like rocks. The mineral exhibit explains how the seemingly dissimilar objects are alike.

Next stop: the Paleo Indian hut. Take the kids by the hand and sit inside the hut. Listen to the recording of a young boy as he shares stories about his life. He sounds so sad because he wishes he were hunting today. Unfortunately for him, baby-sitting for a younger sibling prevents him from joining the older males.

Stroll on over to the Ecology Island and glance through the *Pond Journal*. Drawings and simple facts about fish, frogs, dragonflies, and other pond creatures fill the pages of the book.

Move on to the working beehive to find the queen bee. You'll discover that this task requires a group effort. As the queen is not alone, you must look for her surrounded by worker bees—like the spokes of a wheel. She is identified by her size, being larger than the workers.

For best results at the Water Station, grab a partner and start turning the handles. Don't be lazy! Watch as water moves up the Archimedes' screw, a simulated process fashioned after an ancient method to raise water into their irrigation system. The energy you and your helper produce determines how much water the crops get.

Take a break from watering the crops, and find the Street of Shops. Ever wonder what shopping was like in premall days? This avenue of mock storefronts presents a delightful look at a late-1800s toy shop, photography studio, and general store.

Need a dental filling while you're in town purchasing a few supplies? Look for the sign in the shape of a tooth over a door. The cost of a filling by Dr. J. H. Wible is determined by the amount of gold he uses.

In one corner of the Street of Shops, an HO scale model-train display runs throughout the day. This exhibit depicts historic sites of the Pennsylvania Railroad as it once traveled through Stark County in the 1930s.

Want proof that the earth rotates? Then, stop in the lobby before you leave and watch the Foucault pendulum as it swings back and forth over a five-foot area on the floor. Be patient. Every eight to ten minutes, the steel sphere knocks down two opposite pegs, from a circle of 120 pegs that are evenly spaced around a compass.

The Museum of History, Science and Industry

Discover World shares building space with the Museum of History, Science and Industry. Wander into the McKinley Room, where you'll see the world's largest collection of William McKinley memorabilia. Listen as two mannequins play the roles of President McKinley and his wife, Ida. The two characters engage in a lifelike conversation discussing topics of the day, such as the Spanish rule in Cuba and the personal sadness they feel at the loss of their young daughter, Katie.

Before departing this museum, weigh yourself with the suction of a Hoover vacuum cleaner in the museum's Industrial Hall. You'll also find antique milk containers, a display commemorating Mr. Bell's telephone invention, and exhibits that focus on the multi-international industries of Stark County.

A President's Tribute

McKinley National Memorial

Heavy bronze doors lead to the inside of the pink granite monument dedicated to the twenty-fifth president of the United States. A double sarcophagus holds the remains of William McKinley and his wife. In the rear wall of the rotunda, the couple's two young daughters are entombed.

Look high above the sarcophagus to the red, white, and blue dome. Forty-five stars represent the states in the union when the monument was built in the early 1900s.

This impressive tribute to the assassinated president stands in the midst of a wooded park with bike paths and picnic areas, overlooking downtown Canton. As you climb the 108 steps to the monument's entrance, take a break near the statue depicting McKinley delivering his last speech.

Entry to the monument is handicapped accessible from the rear of the memorial.

Other Canton-Area Attractions

- Take a tour of the only known vacuum-cleaner museum in the world, the Hoover Historical Center. The restored Victorian farmhouse was the boyhood home of William H. Hoover, founder of the Hoover Company. A large collection of memorabilia, plus antiques and early cleaners, fills the museum.

- Touchdown! The Pro Football Hall of Fame features four connecting galleries curved around a football-shape dome. Fans of all ages enjoy the Super Bowl memorabilia, the Twin Enshrinement Halls, and the popular movie theater. Visit the museum store for your favorite football souvenir.

- Love those classic cars? Check out the Canton Classic Car Museum. You'll discover more than thirty-five vintage models in this little museum of nostalgia.

- The Cultural Center for the Arts is truly an outstanding complex. It houses the area's major art attractions: the Canton Museum of Art, Canton Ballet, Canton Civic Opera, Canton Symphony Orchestra, and Players Guild of Canton. Programs and special events are offered throughout the year.

- Stark County holds the distinction of being "Ohio's Golf Capital." More than three dozen private and public courses within a twenty-mile radius attract golfers of all levels.

Ohio Presidents

Ohio is proud of the fact that more presidents were born or raised in this state than in any other. Many of the presidential homesites and monuments offer tours and special events.

- William McKinley lived in Canton; however, the city of Niles was his birthplace. The National McKinley Memorial Library and Museum features presidential campaign items, rare documents, personal papers, and Spanish American War memorabilia. Call 330-652-1704.

- The Rutherford B. Hayes Presidential Center (419-332-2081) in Fremont features a stately thirty-three-room mansion, a museum, library, and a wooded estate.

- The only memorial to the nation's twenty-seventh president is located in the Mount Auburn section of Cincinnati. Call the William Howard Taft National Historic Site at 513-684-3262.

- Ulysses S. Grant's Birthplace (513-553-4911) can be found near the banks of the Ohio River in the town of Point Pleasant. The three-room frame cottage is open to the public.

- The Warren G. Harding Presidential Home and Memorial (740-387-9630) is located in Marion. President Harding conducted his famous "front-porch" campaign at this residence. The Memorial is a short drive from the Harding home.

- View the final resting place of President William Henry Harrison at the Harrison Tomb State Memorial in the town of North Bend (513-941-3490). North Bend, located in the southwestern corner of the state, was the residence of both the nation's ninth president, William Henry Harrison, and his grandson, Benjamin Harrison, the twenty-third president.

43

A President's Tribute

FOR MORE INFORMATION

For further information, contact the McKinley National Memorial and McKinley Museum of History, Science and Industry, 800 McKinley Monument Drive Northwest, Canton, OH 44708; 330-455-7043. Hoover Historical Center, 1875 Easton Street Northwest, North Canton, OH 44720; 330-499-0287. Pro Football Hall of Fame, 2121 George Halas Drive, Canton, OH 44708; 330-456-8207. Canton Classic Car Museum, 555 Market Avenue South, Canton, OH 44702; 330-455-3603. Cultural Center for the Arts, 1001 Market Avenue North, Canton, OH 44702, 330-452-4096.

Or contact the Canton/Stark County Convention and Visitors Bureau, 229 Wells Avenue Northwest, Canton, OH 44703-2642; 800-533-4302 or 330-454-1439. Website: www .visitcantonohio.com.

Northeast

9

Buzzards and More in Medina County

EACH YEAR ON MARCH 15, A PACK OF HARDY, CURIOUS SOULS heads for the cornfields at Hinckley Reservation. Their mission: to await the return of the buzzards.

Like clockwork, the buzzards appear at the park in search of food. Rocking and tilting their six-foot wings, the large, two-toned, blackish birds are visible for several miles on a clear winter's morn. The reservation, part of the Cleveland Metroparks system, features a combination of rock ledges, open fields, and forests. It provides an ideal nesting ground for the buzzards (also called turkey vultures).

On the weekend following March 15, a traditional Buzzard Sunday celebration occurs. If March 15 falls on a Sunday, the fest is held that day. Naturalists and rangers answer questions and share buzzard tales, a pancake breakfast is served, and area crafters sell their wares at a show.

You may well ask, "Why Hinckley?" Local folklore suggests several unconfirmed theories. Perhaps, some authorities say, the buzzards were attracted to the piles of refuse and unwanted game after the Great Hinckley Varmint Hunt in 1818. A Hinckley Chamber of Commerce brochure reads: "At that time, 475 men and boys lined up along Hinckley's twenty-five-mile-square perimeters and began moving inward, in one of the largest drives in history to rid an area of predatory animals destroying local farm stock." Another popular theory mentions "vultures of the air" at the gallows of the Big Bend in the Rocky River where the Wyandot Indians had hung a squaw for practicing witchcraft.

Whatever the reason, buzzards are a big deal with the townsfolk in Hinckley. Perhaps you might want to check out the big birds next March. Be there early, as the first buzzards usually appear around 6 A.M.

The Valley City Frog Jump

Eight-year-old Jimmy prefers his pet frog to buzzards.

"Come back here!" he scolded, as the frog escaped from his hands and leaped away.

Jimmy looked around as the other contestants readied themselves for the race. His favorite pet, named Sylvester, was competing in the Valley City Frog Jump.

If your kids own a pet frog, let them bring it to the competition. No frogs in the family? Not to worry. The little critters can be rented for the heat.

"The competition is fun to watch, especially with the little kids and their frogs," said Dan Hostetler, Medina County Convention & Visitors Bureau. When the annual race is finished, Dan suggests that visitors "find the old-timers and listen to their stories about catching frogs."

A steak, potato, and corn dinner is served after the competition.

And what about Sylvester? Good news! Jimmy managed to catch him before the race started. He won a trophy for placing second.

More Medina County

Medina County, located approximately twenty minutes south of the metropolitan Cleveland area and twenty minutes west of Akron, draws buzzard watchers and frog-jump competitors each year. But, says Hostetler, the main attractions are "the agriculture, the greenhouses, and the farm markets." Spring and fall are the busiest.

Looking for a rare plant variety? The Lafayette Green House, in the town of Medina, specializes in hard-to-find and older plants.

If your timing is right, catch a glimpse of the bison roaming freely at the Whitefeather Bison Company in Wadsworth. Chemical-free luncheon meats and thirty different bison-meat cuts are sold over the counters of the hand-built log cabin owned by the company.

Bring your appetite to the Johnny Appleseed Festival held during the third weekend in September. Succulent barbecued ribs are soaked with a sauce made with apple butter. The Mapleside Farms complex in the town of Brunswick hosts this autumn event. Kids love the hay mazes, hayrides, and homemade ice-cream choices.

The year-round farm operates a full-service restaurant overlooking a valley of five thousand apple trees. Bag your own apples from the mix-and-match bins.

Shopping, anyone? More than two dozen antiques stores, scattered throughout the county, hold a variety of primitive pieces and collectible treasures. For a well-deserved shopper's break, sip some tea at the Victorian-inspired Miss Molly's Tea Room in the town of Medina, or revive your spirits with a cup of cappuccino at one of several area coffee shops.

Buzzards and More in Medina County

For More Information

For further information on area events and attractions, contact the Medina County Convention & Visitors Bureau, 124 West Lafayette Road, Suite 100, Medina, OH 44256; 800-860-2943 or 330-722-5502. Website: www.junior.apk.net\ ~mccvb\.

For buzzard details, contact the Cleveland Metroparks, 4101 Fulton Parkway, Cleveland, OH 44144-1923; 216-351-6300.

Northeast

10

Meet Me in Mespo

THE STEADY RHYTHM OF "CLOP-CLOP-CLOP-CLOP-CLOP-CLOP" suddenly halted as our horse-drawn buggy reached the back-road intersection.

"Whoa!" said Lester Hostetler, our Amish guide, as he tightened the reins on a horse named Lady.

We exchanged waves with the passengers in the approaching buggy.

"That's my son driving that buggy," said Lester.

It was bleak and rainy as Lester maneuvered the horse along the last leg of our late-afternoon ride. He stopped in the driveway just shy of his farmhouse. Sara, Lester's wife, welcomed us as we stepped out of the back of the Amish buggy.

"Are you hungry?" she asked, as she whisked us into the kitchen and directed us to the table set for two.

Sara had prepared a feast: garden salad with choice of dressing, fried chicken, real mashed potatoes and gravy, stuffing made with homemade bread, and peach or apple pie for dessert. Truly, a Thanksgiving-quality supper!

We sat face-to-face in the dimly lit kitchen as Sara fussed and served the meal. We urged her to share with us the heaping portions of food, but she declined, instead pouring herself a cup of coffee. But she did sit at the table with us. Lester joined the threesome shortly afterwards for conversation.

"I made the stuffing with the homemade bread that Lester baked," said Sara, as we raved about the best stuffing ever. "I also make jams and jellies," she added.

That explained the "Jams and Jellies" sign on the front lawn.

Food disappeared as rapidly as the natural outdoor light slipped away. As darkness surrounded our intimate dinner party, Lester wandered off, found the torch, and lit the kerosene lamp—the house has no electricity.

The Hostetlers, an Amish couple with six adult children and a growing list of grandchildren, live on the outskirts of Mesopotamia, a village of approximately three thousand residents. Seventy percent of the population is Amish. Time permitting and with advance notice, Lester provides buggy rides for Mesopotamia visitors, and Sara cooks a meal.

Reluctantly, it was time for Vicki (my weekend traveling buddy) and me to leave the comfortable Hostetler kitchen, so we said our goodbyes, exchanging lots of warm hugs and handshakes.

Down the road a bit from the Hostetler farm sits the Stone House Bed & Breakfast, the home of Lester and Sara's nephew Sam and his family. The circa-1830s structure, situated on a slight hill, furnishes overnight guests with privacy, midnight snacks, a fantastic (and filling!) breakfast, and some special camaraderie with the non-Amish innkeepers, Darcy and Sam Miller. Children are always welcome at the Stone House.

There are several options for exploring the town that the locals call Mespo. Linda Angstrom, a Yankee (or non-Amish), offers her services as a tour guide. For a reasonable fee, you'll get a wonderful outsider's peek at some of the Amish homes, schools, and farmlands, plus fascinating background information on the town's occupants. She begins her tour at the Commons, an oval-shape "common" plot of land measuring a quarter mile long and five-eighths of a mile around.

This narrow strip was used by the town's early settlers as a grazing area for livestock.

The Commons is also a great starting point for a self-guided tour. Stroll through the End of the Commons General Store, one of several dozen circa-19th-century buildings. This grocery/animal-feed/souvenir store lures paying customers and browsers alike. As you roam about the establishment, note the original wood floors and the eye-catching collection of antiques and outdated grocery items lining the upper shelves. If you're searching for packages of bulk flours or large quantities of spices, or you experience a sudden urge for a chocolate ice-cream cone, you'll find them at the general store.

After you've made your final selections, pile back into the car and head west on State 87. An unhurried ride along the two-lane highway will take you past small wooden shacks scattered in front of simple, vinyl-sided Amish homes. Drive slowly and watch for hand-painted signs: Baked Goods, Jams & Jellies, Maple Syrup, Quilts. Selections are best in the morning hours.

If you venture south of the main road, look for the one-room schoolhouse. Behind the school, near the fence, you'll see two wooden outhouses with painted signs that read "Boys" and "Girls." Cows graze nearby. Continue your journey along the country road. Pastel-colored dresses, identical in their simplistic style, are often seen air-drying on clotheslines.

As we traveled the last stretch of our afternoon jaunt, circling back in the direction of the Commons, we observed several outdoor phone booths that were equipped with loud bells. Telephones are not allowed inside Amish homes.

Our day in Mespo ended with a piercing chill in the air. We didn't really mind. The two companions left town with a renewed awareness for a simpler life.

Roadside stands, some restaurants, and the general store in Mesopotamia are closed on Sundays. Also note that generally speaking, the Amish do not like to have their pictures taken—it is important to respect this.

Black buggies travel along the highways and back roads. *Stay alert* to the slow-moving vehicles.

For information on the Old Stone House Bed & Breakfast, contact Sam and Darcy Miller, 8505 State Route 534, Box 177, Mesopotamia, OH 44439; 440-693-4186. This bed-and-breakfast is the only overnight accommodation in Mesopotamia.

Inquiries on buggy rides and dinner at the Hostetler home should also be made at the Old Stone House. The Hostetlers are not equipped to handle large groups.

Contact Linda Angstrom, 8480 South Girdle Road, Middlefield, OH 44062, 440-693-4459, for Mesopotamia tours. Guided tours are available April through November 15.

Every even-numbered year (2000, 2002, etc.), during the third weekend in September, the town hosts the Mesopotamia Civil War Encampment and Reenactment. Music, food, children's games, and an authentic period funeral highlight the festival. For specific information on this event, call 440-564-2040, twenty-four hours a day.

The city of Warren, forty-five minutes southeast of Mesopotamia, offers a long list of lodging possibilities. To obtain information on Warren accommodations and all area attractions, contact the Trumbull County Convention & Visitors Bureau, 650 Youngstown-Warren Road, Niles, OH 44446; 800-672-9555. Website: www.trumbullcountycvb .org.

52

Northeast

11

Escape to Punderson

IT WAS LATE JUNE. AN IDEAL DAY FOR A HIKE IN THE WOODS. The sun played tag with the clouds as the amateur hikers weaved down and around the path. The ground was soft, the aftermath of a torrential rainstorm. Yet, spirits were high along Punderson State Park's walking trail as the hearty souls trekked through a forest dotted with tall sugar maples and wild black-cherry trees. Markers posted along the pathway provide descriptions of this land once covered with ice. When the buried ice melted, more than twelve thousand years ago, "kettles" (depressions) remained. According to one sign, the ninety-acre, spring-fed Punderson Lake is the largest kettle lake in Ohio.

The park furnishes a haven for diverse vegetation and animal populations. Mallards and sparrows frequent the edges of the lake, building nests in the thick vegetation of the marsh. Great horned owls, muskrat, beavers, white-tailed deer, and raccoon are often sighted within the park's boundaries.

Punderson State Park Lodge features a year-round escape with plentiful options from hectic lifestyles. If you sit on a bench near the slight hill behind the manor house, you'll be treated to a picture perfect view of the lake. An occasional canoe, anglers fishing for bass, perch, sunfish and trout, and kids in rowboats decorate the calm waters.

Summer months entice throngs of beachcombers. Non-lake swimmers cool themselves at the pool, which is situated just a few steps from the English Tudor–style lodge. An eighteen-hole public golf course challenges players of all levels. You can also rent boats and bikes, or bring your own. Only electric motors are permitted on the lake.

When the snow falls, Punderson's guests take advantage of the park's facilities. A lit toboggan run, a sled hill, cross-country paths, and snow trails delight winter enthusiasts. When the weather cooperates during January, two annual events are held: the Ohio Championship Cross-Country Ski Race and the Buckeye Classic Sled Dog Race.

The park and the lake are named after Lemuel Punderson, the township's first permanent settler in 1808. He used the "big pond" as a power source for a gristmill. The family's small estate developed into a popular gathering place. As the years progressed, Punderson Lake provided a quiet resort area with summer cottages and a small hotel. The peaceful setting lured city dwellers to a refuge away from the bustling Cleveland area.

Today Punderson visitors enjoy expanded accommodation choices: fully equipped cabins, comfy lodge guest rooms, and a campground located on the site of a former Indian village. As in the past, the resort attracts crowds who seek a break from their harried schedules.

For More Information

For further information contact the Punderson Manor Resort & Conference Center, 11755 Kinsman Road, Newbury, OH 44065; 800-AT-A-PARK (282-7275) or 440-564-9144. Website: www.amfac.com. Punderson State Park telephone numbers: 440-564-2279 (park office), 440-564-5465 (golf course), and 440-564-1195 (campground).

12

Twice the Fun

SeaWorld and Geauga Lake

The message from the loudspeaker was clear.

"If you sit in the first eight to ten rows, you will get wet. In fact—you will be *soaked*!"

Wiggles and squeals of delight erupted from the front rows in the packed outdoor theater, yet no one moved. It was show time at SeaWorld's Shamu Stadium—featuring killer whales Shamu and Namu!

The gates opened slowly as Shamu emerged to perform center stage. The eight-year-old mammal whizzed through the pool creating whale-size ripples. Cameras flashed. The crowd, hysterical with joy, clapped and waved. Everyone in the Splash Zone was drenched—and loved it.

The killer whale performances are a favorite with Sea-World visitors. Plan to arrive well before show time. It is not unusual for crowds to begin wandering into the stadium thirty minutes or more before scheduled performances.

Animal trainers, wearing their black-rubber wet suits (the man-made salt water registers fifty-five degrees), hang around near the pool after the show to answer questions for the exiting crowd.

"Most of us have a four-year psychology or biology degree," said Jim, an animal trainer. "We use positive reinforcement to teach whale behaviors."

Whales are rewarded with toys, mirrors, and food. If an animal doesn't perform correctly, he explained, "we count to three and start over." Animals are never forced to perform.

"Each whale eats 145 pounds of fish every day. They eat capelin, mackerel, herring, smelt, and salmon."

Shamu's favorite food?

"It's salmon," says the trainer. "These are the big ones, sometimes weighing five pounds."

The park's staff members are extremely knowledgeable and eager to share their animal expertise with guests.

After the whale show, follow the ramps and curvy pathways scattered throughout the park. Look closely to catch a glimpse of the newborn ducklings that cling together near the edge of the stream.

Slip into the Penguin Encounter to watch the more than one hundred polar penguins. Did you know that they sleep standing up with their eyes closed? If you visit during the evening hours, chances are good that the regal, black-and-white-robed animals will be snoozing in the simulated icy Antarctic.

Next stop: the Shark Encounter. The moving walkway inside this exhibit provides fabulous underwater views of the sleek, gray-skinned sharks circling their tank. Look up. Radiant shades of green and orange coral, fish wearing yellow-striped skins, and slippery, smooth eels all share living quarters with the brown, lemon, nurse, and tiger shark varieties. No doubt about it—this walkway is the ultimate in shark watching!

Everything in the Touch Pool near the entrance to the Aquarium can be lightly stroked or picked up. Don't be shy about touching the slimy stingray or the chocolate-chip-colored starfish. Inside the Aquarium, check out the electric eels, rain forest frogs, and some pretty neat giant-size water bugs. An absolute must-see are the moon jellies. These cloudy-colored jellyfish lazily drift with the simulated waves in their glass tank.

Say "so long" to the aquatic life, and consider your options. You might want to search for the harbor seals exhibit. Listen carefully as they hiss, snort, and sneeze. Or let the youngsters stand close to the interactive Dolphin Cove display. Be ready for a bottle-nosed dolphin to poke his head out of the water in search of food from your hand.

Did someone mention food?

Your choices are plentiful in the park: hot dogs, hamburgers, barbecued beef or chicken, fries, and pizza. An Italian full-service eatery and a cafeteria-style restaurant are also available. Or bring your own lunch and have a picnic.

Stay until the sun disappears and let the kids whisper "good-night" to the animals. Then find an open space near the lake, or sit in the bleachers in the stadium. An impressive evening extravaganza bursting with laser stripes and color-coordinated fireworks provides the perfect final touch.

Twice the Fun

Geauga Lake

Adjacent to SeaWorld is a theme park called Geauga Lake. After a hiatus of almost twenty years, I returned to the park on a recent July afternoon. I was impressed. The park glowed, obviously the result of an extensive overhaul by the new management.

For starters, a front entrance complete with a majestic clock tower in a turn-of-the-century motif and a spouting water fountain greeted us. The thrill seekers in the group immediately headed for the roller coaster with the twisted-steel track that rolls over, dives, and spins—and then reverses itself. It's called the Mind Eraser. (I understand it promises a super adrenaline rush.) Looking for more hair-raising coasters? Take your pick. There are currently three more in the park and plans to open a suspended looping coaster named Serial Thriller. Personally, I was content riding the circa-1920s carousel, while I admired the hand-crafted wooden horse that gently raised and lowered me.

Perhaps a river-raft ride that twists and turns through a rocky setting is more your speed. Then, take the family on the Grizzly Run, a white-water adventure that hurls passengers in and around a quarter mile of rapids and small waterfalls.

I watched families do some splashing and sliding at Turtle Beach, the park's water attraction geared for kids. Boardwalk Shores allows big kids and adults an opportunity for endless hours of fun-in-the-water activities.

Geauga Lake features more than one hundred rides and attractions. It offers a nice blend of a classic park coupled with high-tech thrills. And, I should add, it's looking mighty grand at the ripe old age of 110 years young!

FOR MORE INFORMATION

SeaWorld of Ohio is located between Cleveland and Akron in the town of Aurora. The park is open from approximately mid-May through Labor Day and on weekends in September. Admission is charged, with rates lower in the evening. Hours vary. Stroller, wheelchair, and locker rentals are available. For further information contact SeaWorld of Ohio, 1100 SeaWorld Drive, Aurora, OH 44202; 800-63-SHAMU (637-4268). Website: www.seaworld.com. TDD number for hearing impaired: 330-995-2186.

Geauga Lake is directly adjacent to SeaWorld on State Route 43. The park opens in mid-May and stays open through weekends in October. Special fall weekends include the Old World Oktoberfest in September and HallowScream in October. Senior discounts available. For further information contact Geauga Lake, 1060 North Aurora Road, Aurora, OH 44202; 330-562-7131. Website: www.geaugalake.com.

13

Downhill Thrills

LIKE A GIANT SALTSHAKER, MOTHER NATURE SPRINKLES HER powder atop Ohio's steep hills. The snowy stage is set for throngs of skiers who play on the white-capped slopes. But sometimes, the "natural" snowmaker shuts down. No problem for the handful of ski resorts in Ohio. They are all equipped with snowmaking machines.

"If it wasn't for snowmaking, the ski areas wouldn't make it," says Jim Epperson, marketing manager for the Ohio Department of Development, Division of Travel & Tourism. "Snowmaking is vital. By mid-January there are three to five feet of packed snow" from snowmakers.

Ohio's close-to-home ski areas supply a great break for schussers of all ages and levels.

"In five of the six area ski resorts, there is some kind of kids' program for three- to eight-year-olds," said Epperson. In addition, the ski areas have all made an attempt to accommodate the aging-and-active crowd. Snow Trails, he pointed out, "had a great role model: a seventy-something instructor devised a nonaggressive form of skiing that worked well for seniors."

The Buckeye State doesn't need mammoth slopes or mile-high mountains for some quality schussing. There are plenty of options for stay-in-Ohio ski adventures. Here's a brief overview of what's available:

- Snow Trails was the first and is the largest of Ohio's ski areas. The Mansfield-based resort, boasting the highest elevation in the state, has a three-hundred-foot vertical drop and a two-thousand-foot run. Kids' programs include Jiminy Cricket, a service geared for children eight years old and younger. Skiing, instruction, and supervised activities in a gamelike atmosphere make the learning fun!

- A Learn-to-Ski program at Mad River Mountain in Bellefontaine, north of Dayton, lasts six weeks. It includes rental equipment, ski lessons, and a lift ticket. Take the kids to Mad River's Kinder School. They will play in the snow, sip hot chocolate, and (maybe) learn to ski.

- Check out Boston Mills and Brandywine. The two ski resorts, owned by the same company, are located about halfway between Cleveland and Akron. They are three miles apart. Snowboarding is encouraged at Brandywine; it is not allowed at Boston Mills unless Brandywine is closed. Kids receive special attention at both resorts when they participate in Mogul Mites, a program for five- to seven-year-olds; and the Junior Program, for eight- to twelve-year-olds.

- Are you a racer? Clear Fork, nestled in a semicircle of rolling hills in the town of Butler, offers a racing program. Slopes for beginner, intermediate, and advanced skiers are serviced by six lifts.

- Adults sixty-six years and older ski free at Alpine Valley, a resort located just east of Cleveland. If you're sixty to sixty-five years of age, skiing costs half price. Snowboarders are welcome here. Special programs and events include Cub Club (for children six and under); Late Night Madness (reduced rates and a one-hour group lesson), and early-bird specials for morning and afternoon skiers.

So—are you ready for a little downhill action? Then, grab your skis (or plan to rent a pair) and head for the Ohio hills. The snowmakers, with a little help from Mother Nature, have prepared a thick, white blanket for your skiing pleasure.

For More Information

For ski conditions at all resorts, call 800-BUCKEYE (282-5393).

Other contacts: Snow Trails Ski Resort, Possum Run Road, PO Box 1456, Mansfield, OH 44901-1456; 800-332-7669. Mad River Mountain, 1000 Snow Valley Road, Zanesfield, OH 43360; 800-231-7669. Boston Mills, 71 Riverview Road, Peninsula, OH 44265-0175; 800-875-4241. Brandywine, PO Box 597, Sagamore Hills, OH 44067-0597; 800-875-4241. Clear Fork Ski Area, PO Box 308, Butler, OH 44822; 800-237-5673 or 419-883-2000. Alpine Valley, 10620 Mayfield Road, Chesterland, OH 44026; 440-285-2211 or 440-729-9775.

Note: Newly opened resort, Spicy Run Mountain, Woods Road, PO Box 99, Latham, OH 45646; (toll-free) 888-774-2978 or 740-493-2599.

Downhill Thrills

14

City of Murals

STEUBENVILLE

THERE ARE NO THEME PARKS. Overnight accommodations number less than a handful. And barge traffic hauls iron ore and gas to the steel mills along the narrow waterway that separates the states of West Virginia and Ohio. Yet, Steubenville is worth a leisurely Sunday afternoon jaunt.

As you drive through the city (population 22,000), you'll discover more than twenty-five original paintings located behind and on the sides of buildings, tucked in alleyways, and around street corners. Thanks to the right mix of an artist's touch, bare building walls, and a downtown historic district in need of a little spark, an outdoor art gallery emerged. It has become one pleasant alternative to the sometimes-stuffy indoor museum scene.

Converting unsightly walls into mural masterpieces was completed by a host of Ohio and internationally known artists. Each mural portrays an event in Steubenville history. Using scaffolds, ladders, buckets of paint, and brushes, the artists spent weeks and, in some cases, months perfecting their work.

The first mural was painted on the parking-lot side of the World Radio Building. It was completed in 1986 by artist Michael Wojczuk. Entitled *Market Street*, the 60' × 30' painting depicts the main intersection of Steubenville during the early 1900s. The scene is so authentic-looking that it appears as if the viewer could actually run down the street and catch the trolley that is painted on the wall.

The Honor Roll, a 105-foot-long mural on the alley side of a pharmacy, lists names of the men and women from Jefferson County who served in World War II. The artist has painstakingly painted each name on the wall.

Stanton Park remains only a memory for many of the local folks, but the 1901 bustling amusement park survives on the side of the Citizens Banking Building. Look in the background of the *Stanton Park* mural for the wood-frame roller coaster. Did the ladies with the oversize flowered hats and ankle-length skirts ride the coaster? What about the gentlemen with their three-piece suits? Or was the coaster just for kids? Wonder what was so funny at the Laughing Gallery? Note how cleverly the artist painted the park scene around the modern-day automated teller machine.

White Star Market depicts the 1920s-era grocery store owned by the father of sports commentator "Jimmy the Greek" Snyder. Take several steps back. You're looking at a thirty-four-foot-high painting of an indoor market scene. There are shelves stocked neatly with canned goods, bins filled with potatoes, and flour bags stacked on the floor. The painting is best seen from the parking lot adjacent to the visitors bureau.

"The murals are a cohesive historical project. There's a story behind each one. The best way to see them is to have a guide; it means so much more," noted Louise Snider, executive director of the Downtown Business Association.

Get a map. Then walk or drive through the town in search of the art treasures. Small directional signs indicate the location of the murals. For a fee, a guide will accompany you in your car and conduct a two-hour tour.

When you've completed the tour, wander back to the corner of Washington and Fifth Streets near the *1897 Centennial Arch* mural. In addition to the colorful painting on the side of the Elks building, this tiny slice of the city features a car museum and animation factory.

After admiring the arch mural, step inside the 1931 art deco building with attached gift shop that houses the Welsh Jaguar Classic Car Museum. Automobile memorabilia, a 1955 300 SL Mercedes Gull Wing, and some 1960s muscle cars fill the one-room exhibit.

Ever wonder how animated characters are made? Before leaving Steubenville, you can find out at the Creegan Animation Company, the nation's largest manufacturer of animated and costume characters. While you're there, peer inside a headless mechanized body to see how the parts move. Check out the shelves crammed with hundreds of plaster molds shaped like heads, feet, hands, and animals. Tours of the facility are free.

FOR MORE INFORMATION

To find the locations of the murals, stop and get a map or arrange for a tour guide at the Steubenville Convention & Visitors Bureau, 501 Washington Street, Second Floor, Steubenville, OH 43952; 740-283-4935. Or contact the Steubenville City of Murals Office, 740-282-0938, same address, just across the hall on the second floor. If the offices are closed, pick up a brochure on the first floor of the building at the Jaggin' Around Restaurant, 501 Washington Street. Brochures are also available at the downtown Information Center, 141 South Fourth Street.

For information on the Welsh Jaguar Classic Car Museum, contact the museum, 501 Washington Street, First Floor, Steubenville, OH 43952; 740-283-9723.

City of Murals

Contact the Creegan Animation Company for tour information, 510 Washington Street, Steubenville, OH 43952; 740-283-3708. Advance reservations are preferred for the free tour.

Other Steubenville attractions: Jefferson County Historical Museum and Genealogical Library, 426 Franklin Avenue, Steubenville, OH 43952; 740-283-1133. Old Fort Steuben, Adams at South Third Street, PO Box 1787, Steubenville, OH 43952; 740-264-6304.

On the weekend closest to June 7, Dean Martin's birthday, Steubenville plays host to an annual Dean Martin Festival. For details on the fest, call the Visitors Bureau or check out the website: www.ridgefieldgroup.com\deanmartin.

Northeast

15

Circle of Culture

UNIVERSITY CIRCLE

IT'S CALLED A CIRCLE, BUT ACTUALLY IT'S SQUARE. EIGHT
museums, several performing arts organizations, lush gardens, appealing architectural structures, and eclectic eateries
fit snugly within a square mile on Cleveland's eastern edges.

"University Circle is a destination in its own right. Many
attractions are located in proximity to each other. We are
only five miles from downtown Cleveland, so the Circle can
be combined with town for a great weekend," said Whit-
ney Bohan, director of public relations for University Circle
Incorporated.

Let's meander through the streets of this popular slice of
the city and take a peek at its highlights.

- Explore the wonders of the world at The Cleveland
  Museum of Natural History. Prehistoric creatures, planetarium programs, and the Hall of Human Ecology add
  spark to Ohio's largest and oldest museum dedicated to
  natural history. Be sure to take the kids to the outdoor
  display where bald eagles, hawks, foxes, and owls are
  housed in their natural habitat.

- Spend an afternoon viewing works of art from all periods
  and cultures at The Cleveland Museum of Art. The

museum's collections of Asian and medieval Western art, American and European painting, and decorative arts are especially impressive. Free admission.

- Kids just stand and stare when they first encounter the eighteen-foot-high Giant Tooth at The Health Museum of Cleveland. When Juno, the transparent woman, speaks, they listen in awe. This museum, the only institution of its kind in the Western Hemisphere, is committed to providing health science information by means of seeing, hearing, and touching.

- A collection of artifacts, photographs, documents, and paintings is featured at the African-American Museum. Visitors are invited to attend films and lectures to gain insight into the history and culture of people of African descent.

- There are *so* many hands-on activities at the Rainbow Children's Museum & TRW Early Learning Center. Kids pour and pump water, carve riverbanks, pull apart the giant watch, and build bridges. The multisensory environment attracts kids from three to twelve years old— they won't want to leave the place!

- The Western Reserve Historical Society (including Crawford Auto-Aviation Museum) boasts of being Cleveland's history center. It is the largest private historical society in the United States, with extensive collections of furniture, decorative arts and costumes, and regional artifacts. Don't miss the rare collection of Cleveland-built cars.

- The Cleveland Play House facility houses three theaters, a production center, the Play House Club, and the Cleveland Center for Contemporary Art. Established in 1915, it is the nation's oldest professional not-for-profit theater.

- Severance Hall swells with the sounds of the world-renowned Cleveland Orchestra during the winter season. The orchestra performs at Blossom Music Center in Akron during the summer.

FOR MORE INFORMATION

For general information on the University Circle attractions call 216-791-3900.

Other contacts: The Cleveland Museum of Natural History, 1 Wade Oval Drive, University Circle, Cleveland, OH 44106; 216-231-4600. The Cleveland Museum of Art, 11150 East Boulevard, Cleveland, OH 44106; 216-421-7340. The Health Museum of Cleveland, 8911 Euclid Avenue, Cleveland, OH 44106; 216-231-5010. African-American Museum, 1765 Crawford Road, Cleveland, OH 44106; 216-791-1700. The Rainbow Children's Museum & TRW Early Learning Center, 10730 Euclid Avenue, Cleveland, OH 44106; 216-791-7114. The Western Reserve Historical Society, 10825 East Boulevard, Cleveland, OH 44106; 216-721-5722. The Cleveland Play House, 8500 Euclid Avenue, Cleveland, OH 44106; 216-795-7000. The Cleveland Orchestra, Severance Hall, 11001 Euclid Avenue, Cleveland, OH 44106; 800-686-1141 or 216-231-7300.

For information on all Cleveland attractions, contact the Convention & Visitors Bureau of Greater Cleveland, 3100 Terminal Tower, 50 Public Square, Cleveland, OH 44113; 800-321-1001 or 216-621-5555. Website: www.travelcleveland.com.

Circle of Culture

16

Great Lakes Lore

VERMILION

WHEN THE WIND SHIFTS DIRECTION AND MIDNIGHT-BLUE clouds creep over Lake Erie in midday, boaters, beachcombers, and writers seek dry land.

The Inland Seas Maritime Museum, just steps from the churning lake, rendered an ideal shelter from the storm in the coastal village of Vermilion. When we were safely inside the museum's vestibule, we bypassed the gift shop (only temporarily) and set out to explore the mansion that once belonged to Commodore Fred Wakefield, a prosperous community leader. In 1953 the Wakefield family donated the mansion to the Great Lakes Historical Society to be used as a museum.

The museum's exhibits pay special tribute to Great Lakes lore via ship models, paintings, artifacts, and a video presentation. As you stroll from room to room, note the extensive medley of Great Lakes shipping memorabilia, including whistles from famous steamers, ships' telescopes, and pewter dinnerware.

Lake lovers tend to congregate in the Pilot House, a sizable remnant salvaged from the ship *Canopus*. When visitors stand inside this authentic deckhouse, which contains a steering wheel and navigational equipment,

they experience an eerie sensation of actually sailing "on" the mighty lake.

Weather permitting, museumgoers can capture some fabulous views of Lake Erie by standing on the outdoor deck, just around the corner from the Pilot House. Look just beyond your right shoulder: a full-size replica of the 1877 Vermilion Lighthouse stands erect on the museum grounds.

Wander downstairs to the museum's lower level. Here's your chance to examine some unique, hefty pieces of nautical equipment. You can't miss the steam engine from the *Tug Roger*—it's just shy of the steps. This heavy hunk of machinery was brought here before the extension to the original building could be constructed.

Also downstairs is one of the most famous Fresnel lenses in the United States, a Second Order type from a lighthouse in northern Lake Huron. Take a few minutes to examine up close this huge, circa-1874 lens.

While you're downstairs, take a peek at the replica of a captain's cabin, complete with bunk, fan, and a compass. The compass was strategically placed over the bed so that the captain could instantly see if the ship was on course, even while he was resting.

Perhaps your uncle or grandfather sailed on a Great Lakes ship. Or maybe you just happen to be a ship buff. If so, the museum's library (located on the ground level) contains "the largest collection of books, periodicals, drawings, records, and technical materials devoted to Great Lakes history" and is an excellent source of information.

If your timing is exactly on the mark (we happened to be there at the right moment), you could witness a whirling waterspout above the lake. When the air is cold and the water is warm, and vice versa, the weather is ripe for the funnel-shape columns of air and spray. There was a ripple of excitement among those of us who had never witnessed such an awesome sight!

Before you leave the museum, mosey into the gift shop. You'll discover a selection of nautical gifts, videos, and books. There are also some prints and pictures of ships and lighthouses worth framing.

FOR MORE INFORMATION

Vermilion furnishes a haven for summer family-style fun. You'll find boat docks, fishing charters, marinas, parks, and a sandy beach. An 1837 historic district is a popular shoppers' stop.

For further information contact the Inland Seas Maritime Museum, 480 Main Street, PO Box 435, Vermilion, OH 44089-1099; 800-893-1485 or 440-967-3467.

Other contacts: The Friends of Harbour Town, 5741 Liberty Avenue, Vermilion, OH 44089; 440-967-4262. Vermilion Chamber of Commerce, 5511 Liberty Avenue, Vermilion, OH 44089; 440-967-4477. Lorain County Visitor's Bureau, 611 Broadway, Lorain, OH 44052-1803; 800-334-1673 or 440-245-5282. Website: www.lcvb.org.

Great Lakes Lore

17

Wine Lovers Weekend

MANY PEOPLE THINK WINE LOVERS ARE ESPECIALLY FUN AND lovable to be around, even though some act a little silly, and others tell tales. And many agree that the grape tastes great!

"This Riesling would be wonderful with fish!"

"I love the pink one with the bubbles."

Such are the comments overheard by festivalgoers at Vintage Ohio, an annual wine celebration hosted by the Ohio Wine Producers Association. The tradition began in the summer of 1995. The weekend party draws thousands of novice and veteran wine drinkers to Lake County in the state's northeastern corner. Ohio ranks fourth nationally in the number of wineries, sixth overall in production. There are approximately two thousand acres of grapes in Ohio, with 60 percent planted for juice and jelly, and 35 percent for wine.

The festival presents an opportunity for wine makers and the general public to converse in a relaxed, casual atmosphere.

"Here's a picture of my mom and dad. They started the winery," said Peter Ferrante as he proudly pointed to a photo of his parents in the Ferrante Winery brochure.

Ferrante Winery & Ristorante, one of twenty-plus Ohio wineries represented at the festival, produces red, white, rosé, and blush wines. If you like a bubbly taste, try a sparkling wine from the cellars of Mon Ami, a historic winery producing more than two dozen varieties of wine.

As you stroll the festival grounds, mosey on over to any of the wine booths and talk to the pros. Find out what makes a wine taste dry. Is sugar added to the grapes? Should red or white wine be served with pork?

Continue exploring until you reach the tent packed with kitchen appliances and utensils. Just follow your nose—a tantalizing aroma surrounds the canvas covering. Step inside, find a seat, and watch the show. Culinary experts, cooking-school instructors, and gourmet chefs share their special skills with the audience.

"You *must* taste as you cook, or else how are you going to know what the dish is going to taste like?" explained the chef at a recent demo. Then she sipped some pasta sauce laced with Ohio wine.

After the lesson, the audience was invited to taste the warm, made-from-scratch sauce. (It was wonderful!)

When you leave the cooking tent, wander toward the booths where local restaurant reps and food dealers display their made-in-Ohio products. Samples of zesty barbecue mustard spread on a cracker, bite-size smoked-turkey squares, crunchy caramel corn, pepperoni slices, soft bread squares flavored with herbs and wine, and thin pretzel sticks are available.

Ever tasted quail or ostrich? You can purchase these delicacies as well as more traditional cuisine at food booths scattered throughout the grounds.

Kids can crush plump, purple-gray grapes with their bare feet. If they're not into grape stomping, let them ride a pony. However, depending on their age, boredom is a possibility. Little tykes in strollers appeared content. Teenagers were scarce (we had two with us—they were very eager to leave). Suggestion: Let the youngsters stay at Grandma's house for this fest. Promise them a future trip to an Ohio attraction geared more for kids. Perhaps SeaWorld, Geauga Lake, Cedar Point, or Kings Island would be more to their liking.

Take a Tip Before You Sip

The Ohio Wine Producers Association offers the following tips to festivalgoers:

- Buy tickets in advance. They will be sent by mail. You will save money and avoid standing in line.

- Bring a blanket. Purchase lunch; open a bottle of wine; and listen to live jazz, blues, rock, or reggae performances.

- Don't sample every wine. There are at least twenty wineries serving more than 150 varieties of wine. It's impossible to sample every wine and truly appreciate them. Decide what type you prefer: red or white; sweet or dry.

- Swirl, sniff, and taste. Hold the wine up to the light; sniff it; take a sip; hold it in your mouth, and swish it around. When you're finished, spit it out in a spittoon. (Go ahead, it's OK to spit. It's all part of the wine-tasting tradition.) You'll stay sober and keep your taste buds fresh.

- Designate a driver. Vintage Ohio offers designated drivers a discounted ticket and free nonalcoholic beverages for the day. Designated drivers are not permitted to sample wine.

For More Information

Vintage Ohio is held in Lake County. For festival information and information on all Ohio wines, contact the Ohio Wine Producers Association, PO Box 157, Austinburg, OH 44010; 800-227-6972 or 440-466-4417. Information on accommodations and area attractions can be obtained by contacting the Lake County Visitors Bureau, 1610 Mentor Avenue, Suite 2, Painesville, OH 44077; 800-368-LAKE (368-5253) or 440-354-2424. Website: www.lakevisit.com.

Wine Lovers Weekend

Northwest

18

Say "Yes" to Bellevue

LOCATED JUST TWENTY MINUTES SOUTH OF LAKE ERIE, THE town of Bellevue invites visitors to explore its backyard. Here are some promising possibilities for travelers interested in nonlake activities. Let's begin with an underground hike.

Seneca Caverns

In 1872 two youngsters tumbled into a hole leading to an unexplored cave on a farm owned by the Good family. The kids managed to pull themselves out and spread the word about their new discovery. Farmer Good allowed the curious townspeople to explore the upper four cave levels on his property free of charge. In 1933 the property was purchased by Don Beel, and it still remains in his family.

Ironically, the dimly lit, easy-paced tour of the natural gray-brown bedrock in Seneca Caverns left us energized. The belowground adventure, just minutes southwest of the city of Bellevue, leads casual spelunkers through seven levels of twisted layered rock, narrow passageways, and low-hung ceilings.

Be prepared to bend and climb. On the lowest level accessible to the public, one hundred feet below the earth's surface, a crystal-clear river flows through the cave. The source is unknown.

Look for the stalactites, icicle-shape formations hanging from the ceiling. Geologists speculate that the formations would be larger if early cave visitors had not broken off pieces of the crystals.

The cavern tour is mildly strenuous. Twists and turns sometimes require holding on to the cave walls—or a nearby companion. Few railings are provided. Unless health reasons prevent it, the cave should not be missed.

Sorrowful Mother Shrine

The Sorrowful Mother Shrine dates back to the year 1850 when a tiny, red brick chapel was used as a prayer and meditation refuge. Today, nestled in a 120-acre woodland south of Bellevue, the shrine has blossomed into a popular indoor/outdoor house of worship. It is one of the first places of pilgrimage in the Midwest dedicated to the Mother of God, drawing persons of all beliefs.

Gigantic oak trees tower high above the grounds. Outdoor stations of the cross, replicas of Lourdes, and sepulchre grottos provide an ideal setting for personal reflection. A religious gift store is open every day, except for certain holidays. Masses are said daily.

Mad River & NKP Railroad Museum

The neatest part of wandering throughout the railroad memorabilia at the Mad River & NKP (Nickel Plate) Railroad Museum near downtown Bellevue is the hands-on policy. For starters, climb aboard the mighty diesel locomotives and pretend you're an engineer. Look inside the mail slots lining the walls of the 1910 Pennsylvania Railroad Postal Car. Check out the wooden ice-refrigerator car built in 1947—a shortage of steel after World War II explains why this railroad car is wood.

A 19th-century depot, a 1940s snowplow, and a lengthy collection of well-kept train treasures decorate the museum grounds.

Oh, yes, if you happen to have a true-blooded train watcher in your group (we did), chances are good you'll spot train traffic passing within yards of the museum. Be prepared with your scanner, and keep the camera handy.

Historic Lyme Village

When a young Englishman completed his triple-story mansion on the eastern edge of Bellevue, there was more than enough space for himself, his wife, and their ten children. Visitors to the John Wright Mansion marvel at the beautifully restored early-1800s home that graces the front entrance near the driveway to Historic Lyme Village.

Guided village tours highlight the impressive mansion and also include tours of a preserved one-room schoolhouse, log cabins, a post office, a general store, and several barns.

You might want to plan your visit on a weekend when antique cars and old-time music entertain village guests.

Say "Yes" to Bellevue

FOR MORE INFORMATION

Seneca Caverns is open daily from Memorial Day through Labor Day; weekends in May and September through mid-October. Contact Seneca Caverns, Bellevue, OH 44811-9592; 419-483-6711.

Sorrowful Mother Shrine celebrates Mass year-round. For further information contact Sorrowful Mother Shrine, 4106 State Route 269, Bellevue, OH 44811; 419-483-3435.

The Mad River & NKP Railroad Museum is open daily, Memorial Day through Labor Day; weekends only in May, September, and October. For further information contact Mad River & NKP Railroad Society, Inc., 233 York Street, Bellevue, OH 44811-1377; 419-483-2222. The museum is located just south of U.S. 20 on Southwest Street.

Historic Lyme Village, State Route 113 East, PO Box 342, Bellevue, OH 44811, is open June through August, and Sundays in May and September. Call 419-483-6052 or 419-483-4949 for specific times.

The Bellevue Area Tourism & Visitors Bureau, Box 63, Bellevue, OH 44811, has more information on all area attractions. Call 800-562-6978 or 419-483-5359.

Northwest

19

Scream Machine Mania!

CEDAR POINT

IT WAS NAMED MANTIS—AFTER A CREATURE OF THE INSECT world. And, if you dare, stand in line and get ready to accept the challenge of the tallest, fastest, and steepest stand-up roller coaster in the world. You are about to embark on what many riders claim to be "the ultimate scream-machine thrill."

Cedar Point, an amusement park/resort in Sandusky, boasts a lengthy collection of roller coasters. In 1892, the park's first coaster was built along the shore of Lake Erie. The Switchback Railway stood twenty-five feet tall and traveled about 10 mph. Mantis, Cedar Point's 1996 addition, reaches speeds of 60 mph, with a 145-foot-tall first hill and a fifty-two-degree, 137-foot drop—all while passengers are standing up!

A dozen roller coasters are only part of the park's attraction. Guests who prefer a more subdued experience are invited to live stage shows, marine-life presentations, a water park, a beach, miniature golf, and go-carts—whew! It's easy to see why Cedar Point regularly receives votes as the "best amusement park in the world" and as the "favorite amusement park in North America."

Let's hear it from the experts—the parents and kids who have been there:

"I'm sure my heart stopped. It was a strange and scary feeling. Of course, I like roller coasters, and the Mantis was absolutely the best. I would do it again!" said thirty-something Theresa.

Mantis is definitely a popular coaster with the crowds, but many patrons rave about Raptor, an inverted roller coaster. It flips passengers over, spirals them upside down into a 180-degree roll, and then repeats the twisting movement in the reverse order.

"If you like roller coasters, Cedar Point is well worth the trip. I went on the coasters—they are awesome. The Raptor is the best if you sit in the front car. It's my favorite. There's nothing in front of you or below. You are suspended. You are hanging," said Dan, a sixteen-year-old high schooler.

Margaret, a fifteen-year-old, describes her nine-hour visit: "I went with the freshman class from my school. I liked going on all the rides—the rides are the best. I did go on the Raptor. My feet dangled; that was really fun. I also like the water rides because on a hot day, it cools you off."

Young Danny, a four-year-old, remembers his Cedar Point visit: "I rode on every ride and liked every ride. I wasn't scared. I want to go back."

Nancy, Danny's mom, explains: "He went on all the *kiddie* rides!"

For More Information

Cedar Point is located on a Lake Erie peninsula, midway between Cleveland and Toledo in Sandusky. Overnight accommodations are within walking distance of the park.

Challenge Park, an activity complex adjacent to Cedar Point, has a go-cart raceway, two eighteen-hole miniature golf courses, and RipCord, a ride that features a 150-foot tethered free fall. A new, monster thrill ride called Power Tower debuted in the summer of 1998. The 300-foot-tall, steel superstructure sends riders up and down at a speed of 50 mph, all in three seconds.

Soak City water park, also adjacent to Cedar Point, offers a variety of sliding and gliding attractions. A "kids-only" pool, filled with fountains, sprinklers, mini slides, and chutes, is centered around a giant steam train.

Both Challenge Park and Soak City are open to the general public—admission to Cedar Point is not required. Each attraction requires a separate fee.

For general information on Cedar Point, Challenge Park, and Soak City, contact Cedar Point, One Cedar Point Drive, PO Box 5006, Sandusky, OH 44871-5006; 419-627-2350. Website: www.cedarpoint.com.

Scream Machine Mania!

20

An Island Paradise

KELLEYS ISLAND

LAKE ERIE ISLANDS COME IN ALL SIZES. KELLEYS ISLAND, THE largest of the freshwater islands in U.S. territory, is only four square miles. Yet, the possibilities are endless as a couple's escape, camper's delight, or family weekender.

Park the car on the mainland in either Marblehead or Sandusky and journey by ferry across the teal blue lake. Once you arrive on the isle, it's a matter of personal taste when it comes to transportation. Options include bicycles, walking, electric or gas-powered carts, and tram tours.

Casual and unhurried depicts the island's pace. Musical tones drift from the family-style taverns; blue-jeaned waiters serve lake-caught perch; and a man of the cloth leads a Sunday-morning service in his tennis shoes. Browsers are welcome at the downtown boutiques.

Tell the kids they're going to play "amateur geologist." Then head for the northern end of the island. Here you'll examine the world's largest display of glacial grooves, left by the mighty Wisconsin glacier. Stroll the pathway surrounding the fenced-in Glacial Grooves State Memorial. A series of plaques relates clues about the evolution of this massive 440' × 35' limestone bedrock. A word of caution: The steps and the platform areas around and over the grooves can be slippery. Hold on.

Look over your shoulder to the land paralleling the grooves. A huge, inactive limestone quarry covers the valley floor. Elsewhere on the island, several active limestone quarries flourish.

Take a hike. But first, pick up trail maps at the Kelleys Island State Park office. The North Shore Loop Trail reveals remnants of an obsolete quarry. You'll discover an 1888 loader used to load crushed stone into railcars, foundations from buildings used to house quarry workers, and a large, man-made hill built to provide access to the stone crusher. While you're on the trail, look for the keeled bud on an Ohio buckeye tree. The Ohio buckeye, which grows sixty to eighty feet high and two to three feet in diameter, is the state tree.

Save time to explore the East Quarry Trail. This path leads hikers past wetlands and a lake filled with smallmouth bass. Be on the lookout for fossil remains of the marine invertebrate animals that lived in the Devonian Sea, 350 million years ago.

After your easy-paced hike, wander back to the paved road and look for the winery. Kelleys Island Wine Company is a delightful discovery. Wine tasting, combined with an emphasis on family recreation, provides a break from golf cart backseats and bicycles. A small tasting room offers the over-twenty-one crowd a chance to purchase samples, a glass, or a bottle of several excellent wines. Try the Vignoles, a classical dry and fruity white wine, or Sunset Pink, a crisp blush wine. For the non–wine drinker, soft drinks and lemonade are available.

Let the kids work off some steam in the children's play area. Nearby, parents sit outdoors, nibbling on cheese, apple slices, and French bread. Volleyball games and horseshoe matches keep the teenage crowd entertained. Picnics are encouraged at the winery. On weekends in the summer, buy a brat and cook it on the grill.

As the sun begins to set, bikes and carts are returned to the rental stands. The ferryboat horn signals a short blast, reminding island visitors that it's time for the day's final trip back to the mainland. Those who come prepared with a toothbrush and a change of clothes for a sleepover on the island can rent a cottage or book a room in one of several 19th-century Victorian inns. Condo rentals and modernized campground sites are other overnight options.

FOR MORE INFORMATION

Two companies provide boats that depart from Marblehead for Kelleys Island. They are Neuman's Kelleys Island Ferry, 800-876-1907 or 419-798-5800; and Kelleys Island Ferry Boat Lines, 888-225-4325 or 419-798-9763. Ferries and cruises from Sandusky include *The Goodtime I*, 800-446-3140 or 419-625-9692, and the *Island Rocket I and II*, 800-854-8121 or 419-627-1500. The two Marblehead ferries transport cars and people. The Sandusky ferry and cruise lines are passenger only. Schedules are subject to change. Always call first before making plans.

Other contacts: Kelleys Island Chamber of Commerce, 130 Division Street, PO Box 783, Department BN, Kelleys Island, OH 43438; 419-746-2360. Sandusky/Erie County Visitors & Convention Bureau, 4424 Milan Road, Suite A, Sandusky, OH 44870; 800-255-ERIE (255-3743) or 419-625-2984. Website: www.buckeyenorth.com.

An Island Paradise

21

A Summer Playground

LAKESIDE

THE KIDS MIGHT BALK AT THE SUGGESTION OF A WEEKEND TRIP without fast-food eateries, familiar chain-hotel lodging, and amusement-park scream machines. "No way, Dad!" "Forget it."

Pay no attention and insist on an open-mind policy. Then pack the suitcases, gather the family, and point the van in the direction of Ohio's northern coastline to the community of Lakeside.

A gray wooden entrance-gate trimmed with white lattice welcomes returning vacationers and first-time curiosity seekers to a summer playground packed with invigorating family-style activities. Balmy breezes roll in from the Sweet Sea, the name coined by Native Americans for Lake Erie. Narrow streets, dotted with a mix of Victorian, Gothic Revival, Italianate, and Second Empire architecture, set the stage for a Chautauqua-like experience. Posted speed limit: 20 mph.

There are several options for exploring the town. Park your vehicle and join the throngs of walkers, or rent a bicycle and ride through the streets.

The lakefront draws crowds of all ages. Toddlers design sand castles and splash in the wading pool. Teenagers congregate with their peers, soaking up the sun and making plans for an evening rendezvous.

"We have a theater that shows up-to-date movies. There are dances once a week in the Pavilion. And teens play basketball and volleyball in the evening at the lighted courts," said Keith Addy, director of marketing for the Lakeside Association.

Not in the mood for lake swimming or suntanning? Park benches are plentiful along the shore. Sit for a spell and listen to the methodic lapping of the waves. Let your mind wander back to the late 1880s when steamboat travel across the churning Lake Erie was a popular means of transportation. From 1887 until the early 1930s, the Lakeside & Marblehead Railroad competed with steamships as a means of transporting passengers to this getaway resort.

Shuffleboard is a *really* big deal at Lakeside. Whether you're a first-time participant or an experienced player, everyone is encouraged to give the game a try.

"We offer shuffleboard and tennis lessons free. There are twenty-six courts. On weekends people have to wait in line," said Addy.

Learn to sail; fish for perch and white bass off the dock; or rent a nonpowered boat. There are no docking facilities for powerboats.

Stroll the two-block downtown shopping district in search of gifts, antiques, books, and souvenirs. Treat the kids to a handful of penny candy or an ice-cream cone.

Rumor has it that the Abigail Tea Room on West Third Street dishes out a mighty good slice of Mississippi Mud Pie. Watermelon Place (decked with watermelon trinkets) serves homemade turtle cake, watermelon juice, coffees, and teas.

In keeping with Lakeside's mission to provide a "family-oriented retreat center specializing in nurturing family growth and interpersonal relationships for people of all persuasions," the town offers inspirational activities as well as social experiences.

Hoover Auditorium, a mammoth facility with seating capacity for three thousand people, hosts a variety of entertainment options which range from jazz concerts and Shakespearean drama to puppet shows and first-class symphonies.

The Heritage Hall Museum provides rainy-day browsing. The one-room exhibit, the former site of Lakeside's first church, is filled with community artifacts and old photographs. This is a great place to soak up tidbits about the town's history.

Lakeside was founded in 1873 by Methodists and the community continues to maintain a strong relationship with the church. The Lakeside Association owns the land. Leases are given for ninety-nine years to resident home owners.

Hairdos and clothing styles have changed since the days of steamships and rail traffic, but the resort's popularity remains the same.

"It is our desire to have a wholesome family entertainment facility," adds Addy.

For More Information

Lakeside is located on the Marblehead Peninsula, almost halfway between Toledo and Cleveland. An admission fee to the grounds is charged beginning the last Saturday in June through Labor Day. Quiet hours are enforced between 11 P.M. and 7 A.M. daily. There are no bars or taverns. Alcohol is not permitted on any Lakeside Association property. For information contact the Lakeside Association, 236 Walnut Avenue, Lakeside-Marblehead, OH 43440; 419-798-4461.

95

A Summer Playground

22

Linger in Lima

JUST FOR AN AFTERNOON, LET'S PLAY "PRETEND."

In order to do this, we're going to head for Lima (say: LY-muh), a city midway between Toledo and Dayton on Interstate 75. Find the American House on North Main Street. This downtown restored 1890s relic features an interesting activity center called WorkPLAYce. Wander inside and sign up with other visitors as part of a fictitious work experience.

For starters, you'll want to join the Lima Locomotive Works shop crew. Remember, this is a make-believe situation. To better help you understand your task, consider the fact that Lima was the junction point for five major railroad freight and passenger lines during the early 20th century. The Lima Locomotive Works established itself as the third largest producer of locomotives during its heyday.

Now, for your assignment: assemble a locomotive from a color-coded blueprint. Teamwork is the key element as you and your fellow workers put heads together in a mock-1940s factory shop.

"Does anyone know where this wheel belongs?"

"Where should I put this red piece?"

Hopefully, after the giggles and a "let's-work-together" approach, your crew will be beaming at the twenty-foot-long replicated locomotive, all in one piece. Nice job!

So, are you ready for your next task?

Let's try your skills at running a 21st-century global music company. How will you promote a world concert tour?

As background, you'll learn that each of the continents involved poses a different problem: Europe is experiencing a major transportation strike; tickets aren't selling in Asia; and Africa is boycotting the concert. Just one more obstacle: the lead singer refuses to sing.

What solution will your task force recommend in order to satisfy every kink in the "World Beat 2010" music tour? Multimedia computers are provided to help solve the dilemma. Remember, teamwork is of the essence. Will the concerts go on, or will they be canceled?

WorkPLAYce is geared for adults and kids ages ten years and older. The entire experience takes two to three hours to complete. Be sure to call ahead to reserve a spot.

Lots More Lima

- The Allen County Museum, located on West Market Street, overflows with a potpourri of local historical artifacts. Steam and electric railroad memorabilia, fire-fighting equipment, mineral and fossil displays, a turn-of-the-century barbershop, and a doctor's office are nicely exhibited in the museum's rooms. An impressive $10' \times 15'$ model of George Washington's Mount Vernon deserves a close-up look.

- The MacDonell House, an elegant three-story Victorian mansion situated next door to the Allen County Museum, was constructed in 1893. The home changed owners several times. In 1960 the last residents, Mr. and Mrs. James MacDonell, donated their showy home to the Allen County Historical Society. Records indicate that Mr. MacDonell prospered as an oilman and a petroleum geologist.

  Seventeen rooms are open for viewing. As you stroll through the two floors that are open to the public, take note of the leaded-glass windows and doors and the cherry and mahogany hand-carved woodwork.

"This room was for 'Men Only'," explains the guide as she leads the group into a large paneled trophy room.

Guns, rifles, and big-game animal heads reflect Mr. MacDonell's love for hunting trips to Africa, British Guiana, and Alaska.

Be sure to roam upstairs before you leave and see the elaborate sitting rooms and bedrooms. Kids love the collection of toys and dolls that are tucked into corners and scattered about the room.

- So—you've worked up an appetite from your trek through the streets of Lima. It's time to cruise on over to Kewpee, a funky, early-1920s hamburger joint. Order a cheeseburger or two, a frosted-chocolate malt, and a piece of cherry pie "to go." Kewpee claims: the "Hamburg-Pickle-on-Top Makes Your Heart Go Flippity-Flop."

FOR MORE INFORMATION

For information on all Lima attractions, contact the Lima/Allen County Convention & Visitors Bureau, 147 North Main Street, Lima, OH 45801; (toll-free) 888-222-6075 or 419-222-6075. WorkPLAYce requires advance reservations for the sessions: contact American House, Metropolitan Place, 306 North Main Street, Lima, OH 45802; 419-22-HOUSE (224-6873). A fee is charged. The Allen County Museum, 620 West Market Street, Lima, OH 45801, offers free admission; call 419-222-9426. The MacDonell House, 632 West Market Street, Lima, OH 45801, charges an admission fee for vistors twelve years of age and older; 419-222-9426.

23

A Picture-Perfect Peninsula

MARBLEHEAD

WE TOOK TURNS STANDING IN LINE. TWO HOURS PASSED. WE
weren't alone. There were literally hundreds of other curious
(or perhaps a little crazy) souls that waited just as we did.

"Only fifteen minutes from this point," said a volunteer
guide.

We were standing within sight of the Marblehead Lighthouse on a balmy Saturday afternoon in July. Tours are infre-
quent, so we were excited about this rare opportunity to see
the inside of the oldest operating lighthouse on the Great
Lakes.

Lines form early. Travelers from miles around gather on
the Lake Erie shore to get a chance to climb seventy-seven
steps to the structure's platform level. The lighthouse,
stretching eighty-five feet high and surrounded by rock slab
formations, borders the lakeshore village of Marblehead.

Lighthouse lookers wandered around the sun-dappled
grounds, dangled their feet in the cool, choppy lake, snapped
photos of family members posing in front of the lighthouse,
and patiently waited . . . and waited.

At last, the end of the line was in sight. It was our turn to
peek inside. Very, very slowly we climbed the winding stair-
case, savoring every step. Several tiny coves in the thick
walls offered rest stops for those of us experiencing a slight
winded feeling. No one seemed to mind a poky person.

At the top, a narrow walkway surrounds the limestone-and-brick structure. A guide answered questions and pointed to several distant landmarks—Kelleys Island, Put-in-Bay, and Cedar Point. In the 19th century, a lighthouse keeper climbed the steps, just as we did, and lit the round wicks in the thirteen small lamps.

"Take your time," said the guide as we circled the walkway one last time, soaking in the spectacular view.

The trip down the steps was easier. When we reached ground level, we all agreed that the lengthy wait was worth it.

Originally called the Sandusky Bay Light, the lighthouse was constructed in 1821 on the easternmost tip of the Marblehead Peninsula. The structure was built to help boats navigate the rocky, dangerous shoreline entrance to Sandusky Bay. Whale oil, stored in a small tank near the lighthouse, was used to light the thirteen lamps, which emitted a bright flame. Today, a Fresnel lens, weighing fifteen pounds, flashes a green glow every three seconds. On a clear night, the beacon can be seen for more than seven miles.

Even when the lighthouse isn't open, the tip of the peninsula entices travelers. The rocky backdrop hugging the shores provides a peaceful haven for watching boat and freight traffic and gazing at year-round sunsets.

More Marblehead

- The Marblehead U.S. Coast Guard Station, the busiest station on the Great Lakes, welcomes visitors to tour the grounds. Watch lake freighters and barges load quarry stone via overhead conveyers at the dock near the station. Be sure to view the French Fresnel lens. Unlike modern lightweight lenses, this spectacular crystal lens weighs almost fourteen thousand pounds. It provided a guiding light from the Marblehead Lighthouse in the early 1900s. Station Marblehead operates twenty-four hours a day.

- A mini strip of shops, unlike the big city mall scene, lines Main Street in the village. Richmond Galleries, crammed with original paintings, prints, and sculptures, features works by Ohio artist Ben Richmond. Lake Erie scenes and lighthouses are predominant themes. A sweetshop, a café, and stores specializing in Northern Isle sweaters, collectibles, and jewelry add to the coastal charm.

- Sandusky Bay, which opens out to Lake Erie and surrounds the southern shores of the Marblehead Peninsula, serves as a prime fishing spot. Early spring attracts walleye, yellow perch, bullheads, and white bass; the spring and summer months lure largemouth and smallmouth bass, crappies, and bluegills.

- Auto and passenger ferries operate a service across Lake Erie to Kelleys Island from Marblehead. (See Chapter 20.)

FOR MORE INFORMATION

For information on all Marblehead attractions and events, contact the Peninsula Chamber of Commerce, PO Box 268, Marblehead, OH 43440; 419-798-9777; or the Ottawa County Visitors Bureau, 109 Madison Street, Port Clinton, OH 43452; 800-441-1271. Website: www.lake-erie.com.

For information regarding Coast Guard tours, contact the United States Coast Guard, Station Marblehead, 606 Prairie Street, Lakeside-Marblehead, OH 43440; 419-798-4444. Lighthouse information can be obtained from the Ottawa County Visitors Bureau. For ferry service contact Neuman's Kelleys Island Ferry, 800-876-1907 or Kelleys Island Ferry Boat Lines, 888-225-4325 or 419-798-9763.

A Picture-Perfect Peninsula

24

Maumee Memories

THE MORNING MIST HUNG CLOSE TO THE SWAMPY BRUSH AS the threesome stepped briskly along the boardwalk. We took turns stopping, kneeling down on the walkway, and peering into the marsh in search of frogs, turtles, and cattails.

"Every grain of sand on our beach was trucked in. This area of Ohio was part of the Great Black Swamp. It extended south of the Maumee River to Fort Wayne, Indiana. There were no dikes, no canals, no natural sand. The water would just flow," said Patrick Czarny, general manager, Maumee Bay Resort & Conference Center.

A great blue heron appeared around the bend. Lake Erie hid in the distance, but we knew it was within easy reach. We continued our stroll on the two-mile stretch of boardwalk, taking time to read the interpretive signs and capture some wonderful close-up views of the terrain through the oversize telescopes. Red-winged blackbirds, yellow warblers, and pheasants stayed out of sight, but we learned that they are often spotted. Wetlands house more species of wildlife than any other habitat type.

Czarny pointed to the distant trees: "There's a nesting pair of bald eagles out there. In the spring, we had a pair of great horned owls. We came out every day and watched the baby ones grow."

A jogger approached us. "I just spotted four deer," he said as he ran by.

Maumee Bay Resort delivers a laid-back, stress-free getaway for couples as well as families with kids. The resort, Ohio State Parks' newest lodge, is located ten miles east of downtown Toledo. The big city atmosphere is close—in case you feel the urge to make a side trip.

Any season is a good bet for visiting the resort. Lake Erie's lakefront breezes cool summer guests. Inland sailing, canoe and boat rentals, and a fishing charter service satisfy water lovers. Pack the golf clubs and try the eighteen-hole "Scottish Links" course.

Looking for a cure for the wintertime blues? Book a deluxe cottage. Light a fire in the fireplace, catch up on your reading, or take a nap upstairs in the loft. All cottages are equipped with a full kitchen. Rooms in the lodge have balconies or patios, and most provide lake views.

Outdoor enthusiasts glide along the cross-country ski trails that twist and turn throughout the 1,850-acre state park. Or bring your sled or ice skates.

Indoor recreation facilities include a sauna, whirlpools, racquetball/wallyball courts, and a swimming pool. The year-round nature center, staffed by a naturalist, presents interactive displays, a research lab, and viewing windows.

Our morning hike ended in the comfy lobby of the lodge, with breakfast waiting in the nearby dining room.

We asked Czarny to tell us what he thought was the primary reason people visit Maumee Bay.

He summed it up: "There is so much to do: beaches, a golf course, tennis, and shuffleboard. The pools, indoor and outdoor, are used the most. Everything is close together—guests can walk from one activity to another."

For More Information

For lodge and cottage reservations, contact Maumee Bay Resort & Conference Center, 1750 Park Road #2, Oregon,

OH 43618-9700; 800-AT-A-PARK (282-7275) or 419-836-1466. Website: www.amfac.com. Maumee Bay is one of eight Ohio State Park Resorts. For further information contact the Maumee Bay State Park (administered by the Division of Parks & Recreation), 1400 Park Road #1, Oregon, OH 43618; 419-836-7758.

Maumee Memories

25

Add an Island to Your Day

PUT-IN-BAY

THE LINES FORM QUICKLY ON THE DOCK NEAR THE ROCKY shores of Catawba Point. Eager passengers wait for the eighteen-minute ferry ride to South Bass Island. Their destination, more commonly called Put-in-Bay, rests in Lake Erie three miles north of the Ohio mainland.

Summer months lure a mixed populace ranging from the subdued soul to the adventure seeker. Here's a place to take the family, a date, or the grandparents.

Plan to explore the island on foot, by bicycle, or via an electric cart. Automobiles are scarce and unnecessary for a day or weekend jaunt. Bring a bike or rent one. Cart rentals are available, but remember that waiting lists are a common occurrence when the weather cooperates. Rent early or late in the day.

Boats arrive in all shapes and sizes, docking on the island's northern shore. Truly a partygoer's paradise! During peak summer weekends, boaters at the public docks are required to allow other boats to tie on or raft off of their vessels.

Put-in-Bay not only serves as a mecca for boat traffic, but it caters to land lovers as well.

The Main Street island scene, packed with strollers, couples holding hands, and people watchers, swells with commotion as boats and ferries unload their passengers. Follow your nose. Whiffs of simmering chocolate fudge coupled with sweet, succulent barbecued chicken fill the air. Guitar strumming from an outdoor lounge, café-style eateries, Kimberly's Carousel (yes, rides are available), a bakery, and a noisy video arcade keep everyone content.

Souvenir shops stocked with "Put-An-Island-In-Your-Life" T-shirts, miniature replicas of lighthouses, jewelry, pottery, and boat attire satisfy shopping urges. DeRivera Park, paralleling Main Street, provides a cozy backdrop for sharing chicken dinners or a strawberry shake.

Need some refuge from the downtown hustle and bustle? Then, head inland to Heineman's Winery and Cave. "Informal" best describes this watering hole. Sip a glass of wine or grape juice in the outdoor patio. Or nibble on chunks of cheese and crackers. Grab a jacket (the temperature averages fifty degrees) and join the group in Crystal Cave to view the world's largest geode.

Across the road from Heineman's, check out Perry's Cave. Supplies and prisoners were kept here during the War of 1812.

Commodore Oliver Perry captured a British flotilla of six ships just a few miles northwest of Put-in-Bay, forcing the British to take note of a struggling young nation. In 1912, Perry's Victory & International Peace Memorial was constructed in memory of this military battle.

The open-air observation platform, 317 feet above the lake (reached via elevator), provides a spectacular view of South Bass Island and its neighboring isles in Lake Erie. Unfortunately, the combination of more than three dozen steps and the elevator built in the early 1900s is the only way to reach the top of the monument.

On the western tip of the island, an L-shaped boardwalk extends out into the water. Anglers of all ages hang out here, seemingly undaunted by lake spray. The dock also provides a great spot for bicyclists and walkers to take a break.

If you plan to spend the night on the island, your options are plentiful. You'll find bed-and-breakfast facilities, motels, cottages, and a campground.

FOR MORE INFORMATION

Transportation to Put-in-Bay is provided by the following boat lines: Miller Boat Line, 800-500-2421; *Goodtime I* Ferry, 800-446-3140 or 419-625-9692; and Jet Express, 800-245-1JET (245-1538). Island ferry services and an airline, Griffing Flying Service, 419-734-3149, run regularly scheduled daily trips. During the summer months, ferries depart from both the mainland and the island every half hour (weather permitting), with additional evening trips on weekends and holidays.

Weekends during July and August frequently feature sailboat and powerboat regattas. For further information contact: Put-in-Bay Chamber of Commerce, PO Box 250, Put-in-Bay, OH 43456; 419-285-2832. Ottawa County Visitors Bureau, 109 Madison Street, Port Clinton, OH 43452; 800-441-1271 or 419-734-4386. Website: www.lake-erie .com.

Add an Island to Your Day

26

Welcome, Wing Watchers (and Others), to Sandusky!

BUNDLED UP TIGHT IN HOPES OF WARDING OFF THE WICKED winter chill from the Sandusky Bay, a handful of semiserious bird-watchers stood on a pier, looking up at the sky. Their patience paid off: several great black-backed gulls soared overhead.

The shoreline mix of marshlands and deep forests, extending east of Sandusky to Lorain and then west to Port Clinton, has been dubbed Lake Erie's Wing Watch region. An abundant food supply and ideal weather conditions account for the area's year-round attraction for a multitude of bird types. During the spring and fall, more than three hundred species of hawks, shorebirds, gulls, and songbirds migrate here, and more than one hundred of these species will nest in the region.

Wing watching lures experts and novices alike. It's really very easy. A handy field guide, a keen sense of observation, and knowing where to "watch" are all that's needed. Check with the Lake Erie Wing Watch organization for a list of "hot spots," wing-watching hints, and a calendar of bird-watching-related events. Soon you'll be an official Lake Erie Wing Watcher!

More to See and Do in and Around Sandusky

Sandusky ranks as a favorite any-day-of-the-year destination point. Let's examine some of the indoor/outdoor activities appropriate for family fun.

- Walleye, yellow perch, smallmouth bass, catfish, and steelhead trout account for some fascinating fishing adventures. The combo of warm lake temperatures, shallow reef areas, shoals, and rocky island shorelines produces great spawning and nursery grounds for a variety of trophy-size fish.

  Need tackle? Looking for a deep-sea experience? Want to rent a boat? No problem. Charter fishing excursions and boat rentals are plentiful. Or stay on dry land and drop your line from a public pier. If cleaning your catch doesn't appeal to you, pay a fish-cleaning service to do the work.

- There is something wonderfully soothing about the music seeping from the neoclassical structure on the square in downtown Sandusky. Images of childhood carousel rides come to mind. As visitors enter the former post-office building, which is now the home of the Merry-Go-Round Museum, tunes from a blaring band organ fill the air.

  Once indoors, ride an Allen Herschell carousel. Hold on tight! This majestic machine really moves. Then wander throughout the museum on your own or join a guided tour. You'll discover an extensive assortment of carousel-related exhibits. Stop and watch the skillful carver at work. Listen as he describes the process he uses to restore neglected carousel pieces to their original beauty.

  Check out the antique carving shop in one corner of the museum. Workbenches, partially carved animals, and tools offer a close-up peek at an 1867 carousel-making shop. The entire collection belonged to American carver Gustav Dentzel.

Before departing the museum, browse the gift shop. You'll find a nice mix of merry-go-round knickknacks and reading material.

- In the late 1920s, the Sandusky State Theatre opened as a Spanish baroque vaudeville and movie palace. The theater reopened in 1993 after years of community fundraising and extensive renovation. Today, live performing arts and film grace the stage of this grandiose restored landmark.

- Feel like taking a stroll? The Eleutheros Cooke House & Garden association promotes the preservation and restoration of historic buildings and sites. The association supplies brochures for two walking tours. Take your pick. One option is the Downtown Architectural Walking Tour. It takes about one hour. The path weaves through the streets, focusing on dozens of historical sites including a double-ended, side-wheeled ferry in the process of being restored. Mansions done in Gothic Revival, Italianate, and Romanesque Revival decor are highlighted.

Another tour for those who prefer to walk is the Sandusky Downtown Parks Walking Tour, which begins at the statue of the *Boy with the Boot Fountain*. Continue your stroll and discover circa-1840s churches, a courthouse dating back more than a century, and lush flower beds (weather permitting).

- The Sandusky Area Maritime Association operates a compact resource center just a few minutes from the downtown square. If you're interested in nautical artifacts and the preservation of maritime history, stop at the Sandusky Area Maritime Museum on Market Street. Hours of operation are limited.

- Love those scream machines? A trip to Sandusky wouldn't be complete without a roller-coaster ride at Cedar Point Amusement Park. (See Chapter 19.)

For More Information

For information on bird-watching, fishing, and all area attractions, contact the Sandusky/Erie County Visitors & Convention Bureau, 4424 Milan Road, Suite A, Sandusky, OH 44870; 800-255-ERIE (255-3743) or 419-625-2984. Website: www.buckeyenorth.com.

Other contacts: Merry-Go-Round Museum, West Washington and Jackson Streets, Sandusky, OH 44870; 419-626-6111. Sandusky State Theatre, 107 Columbus Avenue, Sandusky, OH 44870; 419-626-1950. Eleutheros Cooke House & Garden, 1415 Columbus Avenue, Sandusky, OH 44870; 419-627-0640. Sandusky Area Maritime Museum, 279 East Market Street, Sandusky, OH 44870; 419-624-0274.

Northwest

27

Tiffin Treasures

THE SIGN ON THE SIDE OF RIVERSIDE DRIVE SAYS "FOWL Crossing Ahead."

Cars slow down. Heads turn. The coast is clear: no ducks or geese in sight, though carefree daytime drives along this tree-lined route often reveal families of fowl waddling across the road.

Down the street and around the slight bend, the circa-1800s Pioneer Mill Restaurant lures town "locals" and transient travelers alike. The mill, paralleling the Sandusky River, provides a relaxed spot from which to begin a leisurely look at Tiffin, a town named after Dr. Edward Tiffin, Ohio's first governor.

If you stop at the Mill, consider ordering a beverage, lunch, or dinner. Before departing the historic restaurant, mosey downstairs to Tinkers Dam. Here you can peek at the mill wheels that drive the generators, furnishing the mill with a significant portion of its electricity.

Just a few minutes from the restaurant, you'll find yourself in the low-key downtown district of Tiffin. The discovery of natural gas in the late 19th century attracted glass companies to this town and its neighbor to the west, Fostoria. The glass factories have closed up shop, yet glass remains a serious business for several of the area's residents.

If you visit Crystal Traditions, you'll be treated to a demonstration by a full-time glassblower. A gallery, an outlet, and a manufacturing facility are open to the public. If you're interested, show up at the shop during hours of operation and you'll get a tour.

For a peek at the behind-the-scenes engraving process, wander several short blocks from Crystal Traditions to King's Glass on Washington Street. Step inside the small showroom. Here you'll discover rows of shelves filled with a colorful mix of plates, stemware, sun catchers, and knickknacks.

"We engrave everything but people. We've done trucks, antique tractors, houses, and trains. Each piece is done by hand," said Dave King, hand glass engraver.

Dave and his father, Clyde King, invite customers to join them in their work area where they demonstrate engraving techniques. There are no scheduled "backroom" tours. Just stop by and ask to watch the fascinating process.

More Tiffin Sites

- Stay in downtown Tiffin (just blocks from King's Glass), and take a tour of the Ritz Theatre. The vaudeville/movie palace, built in 1928, hosts a wide variety of performing arts and community events. Italian Renaissance architecture, garden murals, and a Czechoslovakian crystal chandelier adorn the majestic landmark. For tours of the theater, call and make an appointment.

- Mellow hues of green, blue, lilac, and peach glow in the gorgeous glass display at the Seneca County Museum. After you view the striking pieces in the room decorated with the largest collection of Tiffin glass, it's obvious why the region's past popularity as a major glass producer was world renowned.

  In addition to glass, the Greek Revival mansion houses a potpourri of exhibits that detail the county's history. Check out the toys and dollhouses, tramp art, quilts, and natural-history display. Individuals who prefer to stay on the first floor are urged to watch a forty-five-minute video that describes the museum's contents.

Hours are limited. Be sure to call before making arrangements.

Fostoria—Tiffin's Neighbor

- In 1887 natural gas was discovered in and around Fostoria, a town northwest of Tiffin. Thirteen glass plants operated here at different times. None remains open today. The Glass Heritage Gallery on Main Street showcases a collection of antique glass from the thirteen closed plants. The public is invited. Donations accepted.

- Stay on Main Street and wander just two doors down to Foster Glassworks. Jim Maxwell, a master craftsman, demonstrates glassblowing and engraving techniques on request. While you're watching Jim create, ask him to share his story about his employment at Tiffin Crystal, once a major glass plant.

  "I worked for Tiffin Crystal for thirteen years until the company closed. Luckily, they decided to sell the molds. I bought most of them—four to five thousand," he said.

Tiffin Treasures

FOR MORE INFORMATION

For information on all area attractions, contact the Seneca County Convention and Visitors Bureau, 114 South Washington Street, Tiffin, OH 44883; (toll-free) 888-SENECA-1 (736-3221) or 419-447-5866.

Other contacts: Pioneer Mill Restaurant, 255 Riverside Drive, Tiffin, OH 44883; 419-448-0100. Crystal Traditions,

145 Madison Street, Tiffin, OH 44883; 888-298-7236 or 419-448-4286. King's Glass Engraving, 181 South Washington Street, Tiffin, OH 44883; 419-447-0232. Ritz Theatre, 30 South Washington Street, Tiffin, OH 44883; 419-448-8544. Seneca County Museum, 28 Clay Street, Tiffin, OH 44883; 419-447-5955. Glass Heritage Gallery, 109 North Main Street, Fostoria, OH 44830; 419-435-5077. Foster Glassworks, 103 North Main Street, Fostoria, OH 44830; 419-435-1995.

28

Tooling Around in Toledo

IN THE LATE 19TH CENTURY, EDWARD LIBBEY, FOUNDER OF Libbey Glass, convinced the Toledo populace that cut glass should be bought anytime, not just for wedding gifts. His rationale worked. Libbey's success with glass earned him millionaire status.

Libbey and his wife, Florence, believed in sharing their wealth. In 1901, they donated land and founded The Toledo Museum of Art. Libbey served as the museum's first president for twenty-four years.

The Grecian-style, marble structure is nearly a century old. Tales of the museum's humble beginnings describe the days when staff members roller-skated in the galleries. And why not? In the mid-1930s, the wings were empty and the floors were bare. The museum did not own enough art to fill the rooms. However, as the decades passed, the museum's collections flourished, and now it ranks as "one of the top ten museums in the country, in terms of quality."

Plan to spend several hours strolling through the impressive galleries. You'll discover elegant tapestries dating back to the 1600s hanging on walls.

"The tapestries are very valuable. They were always a more highly valued process, partly because they took so much time to create. It would take years and decades to complete. Mothers and daughters and generations of people would work on these," said our guide as she pointed to the silver and gold threads woven into the gorgeous material.

The museum also has a collection of scrolls that date back thousands of years. Dimmed lights are necessary to preserve the delicate ink on the silk.

Further investigation of the museum reveals treasures from ancient Egypt, Greece, and Rome; a medieval cloister; and art by such masters as Rubens, van Gogh, Monet, Degas, and Picasso.

Libbey believed that the art museum should be free to the public. This same policy holds true today. There is no admission fee.

Tips on Toledo

Art is only one reason visitors are drawn to the Glass City. If you go, be sure to investigate some of the town's other top attractions.

- In 1899, a local furniture dealer donated a woodchuck, launching a progressive chain of events that has resulted in a prominent zoo. The Toledo Zoo, and in particular the hippos' home, ranks as a "must-see-in-Toledo" sight. The only Hippoquarium in the world features the neatest close-ups of hippos at play in their crystal-clear under-water dwelling. Step inside the corridor that parallels the hippo tank. You'll soon find yourself gazing into a pair of huge, droopy eyes.

   After a delightful visit with the hippo clan, check out the living quarters of the cheetahs, giraffes, gorillas, monkeys, elephants, and sea lions. The zoo's aquarium contains forty-thousand-gallon-plus display tanks loaded with multicolored fresh and saltwater fish from all around the world.

   Wow—the transformation of the zoo into a wonderland spectacle happens each Christmas season. Thousands of twinkling lights and lighted animal images are neatly sprinkled throughout the park. Bundle up and take a winter walk.

- Moored on the east side of the Maumee River, directly across from downtown Toledo, is the *S.S. Willis B. Boyer.* The 617-foot retired ship ruled for many years as "king of the lake freighters." Grab the kids by the hand and together explore the memorabilia, photography, and artifacts on this nautical museum.

- Old Number 18 Fire House, a circa-1920 working fire station, is the site of the Toledo Firefighters Museum. Highlights include the 1837 Neptune, Toledo's first fire pumper; hundreds of antique fire toys; vintage fire-fighting equipment and uniforms; and a chronological history of the Toledo Fire Department.

- Cruise the Maumee River or Lake Erie on *The Sandpiper.* The sixty-five-foot-long vessel, a replica of a canal boat, glides under bridges and along the city's shoreline. *The Sandpiper* offers diverse trips: Boo Cruises for kids at Halloween, a river taxi during riverfront festivals, and picnic lunch cruises.

- Play ball! The Toledo Mud Hens, a AAA-level affiliate of the Detroit Tigers, delight baseball fans at the Ned Skeldon Stadium. If you're in the mood to cheer a sport with umpires, stadium vendors, and professional players, buy tickets for first-base seats. Then, after the game, hang around and get some autographs from guys who might soon be playing in the major leagues.

- Visit the Libbey Glass Outlet's new location for an extensive selection of specialty glassware, stemware, mugs, canisters, dinnerware, and accessories.

Tooling Around in Toledo

The U.S. Glass Specialty Outlet carries one of the largest collections of coffee mugs in northwest Ohio, plus an extensive supply of glassware. If your timing is right, you can watch glassblowers create works of art before your eyes.

• Next door to the Libbey Glass Outlet is the new Erie Street Market, a year-round complex that features food booths filled with homemade goodies, spices, meats, cheeses, and more. Limited hours of operation.

FOR MORE INFORMATION

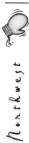

For information on all Toledo attractions, contact the Greater Toledo Convention & Visitors Bureau, 401 Jefferson Avenue, Toledo, OH 43604; 800-243-4667 or 419-321-6404. Website: www.toledocvb.com.

Other contacts: The Toledo Museum of Art, 2445 Monroe Street, Toledo, OH 43697; 800-644-6862. The Toledo Zoo, 2700 Broadway, PO Box 4010, Toledo, OH 43609, 419-385-5721. *S.S. Willis B. Boyer*, 26 Main Street (located in International Park), Toledo, OH 43605; 419-936-3070. Toledo Firefighters Museum, 918 Sylvania Avenue, Toledo, OH 43612; 419-478-FIRE (478-3473). *The Sandpiper*, Harbor Light Cruises, 2144 Fordway, Toledo, OH 43606; 419-537-1212. Toledo Mud Hens Baseball Club, Ned Skeldon Stadium, 2901 Key Street, Maumee, OH 43537; 419-893-9483. Libbey Glass Outlet, 205 South Erie Street, Toledo, OH 43602; 419-254-5000. U.S. Glass Specialty Outlet, 1367 Miami Street, Toledo, OH 43605; 419-698-8046.

Central

29

An Irish Fest and More!

OUTSKIRTS OF COLUMBUS

THE COMMUNITIES WRAPPED AROUND OHIO'S CAPITAL CITY supply getaway opportunities that run the gamut from ceramic and railroad museums to Irish dancing and boutique browsing. Here are some highlights of the towns that border the outskirts of Columbus.

Dublin

Dublin, a straight shot northwest of downtown Columbus, rocks with the sounds, tastes, and traditions of the Emerald Isle during its annual summer Irish Festival. Scones, bangers and mash (sausage and mashed potatoes), soda bread, and Irish stew satisfy hungry partygoers. You can shop for heraldic ornaments, out-of-the-ordinary jewelry, family crests, and Celtic art. Three stages burst with the musical sounds of Irish tunes and lively, foot-tapping entertainment. Youngsters congregate at the Wee Folk area and paint their faces, decorate Irish-style hats, and make potato people using toothpicks and gumdrops.

The weekend closest to Saint Patrick's Day features a parade with traditional pipe-and-drum bands, marching bands, the Grand Leprechaun, and colorful floats. Immediately after the parade, join the revelers for Irish entertainment at the Blarney Bash.

But, don't come to Dublin on Saint Patrick's Day unless you're wearing green. The Keystone Kops "arrest" green offenders and lock them up (just for the fun of it)!

Can't make the Irish celebrations? Not a problem. Dublin's unique outdoor art lures visitors year-round. The sculpture *Field of Corn (with Osage Oranges)* symbolizes Dublin's history as a farming community. Rows of human-size ears of concrete corn stand upright in realistic-looking patterns at Sam and Eulalia Frantz Park. Situated behind the 109 ears of corn, Osage orange trees grow an unusual bumpy fruit the size of a grapefruit.

Other works of public art include *Leatherlips*, a twelve-foot-high limestone portrait of a Wyandot Indian chief, emerging from a sloping hillside; and *Out of Bounds*, comprising seven ten-foot-high sculptures representing soccer balls spread across a field. For a real appreciation of these outdoor masterpieces, get out of your car and get a close-up look.

Central

Worthington

Fifteen minutes north of downtown Columbus is a village named for Thomas Worthington, one of Ohio's first senators, who later became governor of the state. A leisurely walking tour of Worthington showcases the town's historic sites. You'll see a circa-1841 rectory; the oldest commercial building in central Ohio (built in 1808); St. John's Episcopal Church and burial yard, the first Episcopal church west of the Allegheny Mountains; and the Mattoon-Woodrow House, built for Worthington's blacksmith and conductor on the Underground Railroad.

- The restored Worthington Inn, a historic landmark used as a hotel during the Civil War, features fabulous gourmet cuisine and overnight accommodations. Take a peek inside the elegant structure, even if you're not planning to dine or spend the night.

- All abooard! The Ohio Railway Museum offers rides on an outdated streetcar or interurban. More than thirty passenger cars, electric and steam locomotives, streetcars, and interurbans provide a glimpse of the role of transportation in the United States. Hours of operation are limited.

Westerville

In the early 1900s, Westerville had quite a reputation as a "socially clean and morally upright" village. The town prohibition enthusiasts lured the Anti-Saloon League of America to move their headquarters from Washington, D.C., to Westerville.

- The town no longer reigns as "Dry Capital of the World," but the temperance movement is an important segment of Westerville's legacy. Visit The Anti-Saloon League Museum, located in the Westerville Public Library, and learn the intriguing tale of the struggle by prohibitionists. The museum contains original temperance materials, artifacts, and an audiovisual presentation. Guided and self-guided tours are available.

- Time permitting, check out the Ross C. Purdy Museum of Ceramics. Show the kids some of the objects taken into space by an astronaut. Then find samples of high-technology ceramic applications, including space shuttle tiles, automobile engine parts, and replacement joints for

An Irish Fest and More!

biomedical uses. The museum is open to the public on weekdays.

- Otterbein College, a liberal arts institution, produces musicals, children's theater, music concerts, opera, dance concerts, and art exhibits. The general public is invited to attend.

- Shopping, anyone? Tree-lined sidewalks in Uptown Westerville provide a pathway to more than three dozen specialty and gift shops.

- Need a break from your harried schedule? Then, stop and order dessert at the Well-Tempered Quiche—yummy raspberry cheesecake and frozen chocolate mousse are favorites. Or, if you prefer, hang out with the college crowd at Holmes Coffee Station. You can choose from more than twenty coffee varieties (including iced coffee), or munch on flavored biscotti (the almond-chocolate comes highly recommended). You'll feel much more perky.

Central

Other Notable Area Attractions

- Visit Reynoldsburg, dubbed "the Birthplace of the Tomato," during the first week of September for the annual Tomato Festival. Or look for bargains at the J. C. Penney Outlet Center any time of the year. Reynoldsburg is situated on the eastern edge of the Columbus metropolitan area.

- Even if you've never worked on a farm before, join the staff at Slate Run and help with barnyard and household chores. You'll use late-19th-century machinery, implements, and methods at this fully operating, 1880s family farm. Afterwards, gather the family together for a stroll along the nature trails, or enjoy a picnic lunch. The park is located south of Columbus on State Route 674.

FOR MORE INFORMATION

For information on the Dublin area contact the Dublin Convention & Visitors Bureau, 129 South High Street, Dublin, OH 43017; 800-245-8387. Or try their website at www.dublinvisit.org. Dublin Arts Council, Old Dublin Firehouse, 37 West Bridge Street, Dublin, OH 43017; 614-889-7444.

For information on Worthington contact the Convention & Visitors Bureau of Worthington, PO Box 225, Worthington, OH 43085; 800-997-9935. Or visit their website at www.worthington.org. The Worthington Inn, 649 High Street, Worthington, OH 43085; 614-885-2600. The Ohio Railway Museum, 990 Proprietors Road, PO Box 777, Worthington, OH 43085; 614-885-7345.

For information on Westerville attractions contact the Westerville Visitors & Convention Bureau, 28 South State Street, Westerville, OH 43081; 800-824-8461. Or reach them on their website at www.wpl.lib.oh.us/visitors. Anti-Saloon League Museum, Westerville Public Library, 126 South State Street, Westerville, OH 43081; 614-882-7277. Ross C. Purdy Museum of Ceramics, 735 Ceramic Place, Westerville, OH 43081; 614-890-4700. Otterbein College, Westerville, OH 43081; 614-823-1600.

Other contacts: Reynoldsburg Visitors Bureau, 7374 East Main Street, Reynoldsburg, OH 43068; 614-866-4888. Slate Run Living Historical Farm, 1375 State Route 674 North, Canal Winchester, OH 43103; 614-891-0700.

An association called the Central Ohio Heritage Circle supplies information on all of the communities cited here and several other towns in the area. Call 800-297-LOOP (297-5667).

An Irish Fest and More!

30

A Capital City

COLUMBUS

"Columbus is a town in which almost anything is likely to happen and in which almost everything has."

James Thurber

PERHAPS THURBER WAS RIGHT. AFTER ALL, THE AUTHOR'S short stories describe a ghost in his family's dining room, electricity leaking from fixtures, and a heavy front door broken by police.

When Thurber was a student at Ohio State University in Columbus, he lived at 77 Jefferson Avenue with his family and (supposedly) a ghost! If you dare (the ghost hasn't been heard from recently), stroll through the Thurber House, the same house that the author often featured in his writings. After your tour of the 1870s Victorian home, pull up a chair in the dining room (now the Thurber Country Bookstore), and indulge yourself in a short story or cartoon written by the Columbus native.

More Columbus

It's impossible to do justice to the state's largest city during a weekend trip. Believe me, Mom and I tried! Fortunately,

Columbus provides a popular getaway any time of the year. Here's a brief overview of some of its highlights:

- Even before the early risers reach the door to the North Market complex, they know they're in for a special morning treat. The palatable aromas seep through the cracks, filtering out to the parking lot. Come hungry! Once inside, take a deep breath, and savor a potpourri of scents: just-out-of-the-oven baked goods, fresh fruits and vegetables, and brewed coffee. Mmmmm . . . what a wonderful dilemma! Where does one begin? Perhaps the bakeshop is the place to start.

  On a recent Saturday morning, the most popular breads at Tapatio Bread Company were the potato cheddar, a French-style bread loaded with chunks of potatoes and bits of cheddar cheese; and feta, a bread with tomatoes, olives, onions, and feta cheese. Next, why not try the smoked fish, or order a mile-high deli sandwich for lunch?

  "Chocolate raspberry is on tap today," said the woman behind the coffee counter.

  Not really fond of a chocolate-raspberry blend? No problem. More than forty coffee varieties are offered.

  Food choices are endless at North Market, whether you're famished or just craving a snack.

- If you stand anywhere on ground level near the outdoor exhibit at COSI, Ohio's Center Of Science & Industry, you'll probably ask yourself the question: "How the *heck* are those kids able to lift that car?" There's only one way to find the answer: Gather the crew together, go inside the museum, and try it yourself.

  COSI's action-packed center allows visitors of all ages to engage in the process of hands-on science learning. Experience the thrill of a high-wire cycle, crawl inside a windpipe tunnel (yes, a giant-size trachea), or pet a box turtle. Plan to hang around this museum for several hours.

- Need a fast-food break? Stop at the original Wendy's restaurant (opened November 1969) across the street from COSI.

- More than 150 years ago, groups of German-American shopkeepers, carpenters, and brewers settled on the southern end of Columbus. Dubbed German Village, this delightful neighborhood draws masses of people to its lively restaurants and modest shops. The Book Loft (a personal family favorite) is crammed with bargain books in pocket-size connecting rooms. Watch your step as you climb up and down the narrow stairs through an intriguing maze of nooks and crannies.

- The village streets, lined with simple brick homes sporting wood shutters and slate roofs, swell with partygoers during the annual Oktoberfest celebration. Plan a visit during the Haus und Garten Tour for a peek inside the restored homes.

- On the western fringe of German Village, you'll discover a lively historic area called the Brewery District. Crowds are drawn to the eclectic restaurants, a microbrewery, and the live entertainment that fill the 19th-century brewery buildings on South Front Street.

- The Columbus Museum of Art, the first art museum in Ohio, houses more than six thousand objects. The museum is known for several impressive collections: American and European art from 1850 through 1945; 17th-century Dutch and 19th-century French paintings; 19th- and 20th-century sculpture; and Asian ceramics.

135

A Capital City

- Join the crowds on the first Saturday of each month for the "Gallery Hop" in Short North. Trendy shops, eclectic galleries, and nightclubs are scattered throughout this district, located slightly "above" downtown. (You might have to win a lottery if you plan to buy the exquisite glass figurines displayed in some of the stores.) Don't miss Short North—it's *so* much fun browsing and dreaming!

- Ever wonder what the ships looked like that sailed the open seas during the 15th century? The *Santa Maria*, an authentic representation of Christopher Columbus's flagship, is docked downtown on the Scioto River. Tour the ship and learn about the hardships that plagued the crew on its journey to the New World.

Central

- Save some space in your busy day, and schedule side trips to the Columbus Zoo, the third-largest municipally owned zoo in the United States; the Franklin Park Conservatory and Botanical Garden, a huge glass structure featuring unique habitats of the world; and the Wexner Center for the Arts, a complex on the campus of Ohio State University that hosts concerts and performances.

Special Events

- The Ohio State Fair, one of the nation's largest fairs, features big-name entertainment, a spectacular midway, racing pigs, abundant food choices, and lots more. The fair is held in August.

- Sample some of the area's best restaurant dishes at the "Big Bear Rhythm & Food Festival: A Taste of Columbus." Who do you think will win the Best of Taste award? Listen to blues, zydeco (a blend of blues, rhythm, and

Cajun-style), world music, and Dixieland while you enjoy the scrumptious cuisine.

- Catch that patriotic spirit! On Independence Day, the largest parade in Ohio celebrating the nation's freedom travels along Front Street in downtown Columbus. "Red, White & Boom!" is another Independence Day festival, which culminates with "one of the largest fireworks displays in the Midwest."

- Choose from the functional to the fantastic at the Columbus Arts Festival. The downtown riverfront swells with hundreds of artists and craftspersons. Continuous music, gourmet food, poetry readings, and storytelling complement the fest.

    So, now that you've taken a bird's-eye jaunt through the town of Columbus, do you agree with Thurber?

For More Information

Columbus is located at the crossroads of Interstate 70 and Interstate 71. For information on all attractions and events, contact the Greater Columbus Convention & Visitors Bureau, 90 North High Street, Columbus, OH 43215-3014; 800-345-4FUN (345-4386). Or visit their website at www.columbuscvb.org.

Other contacts: The Thurber House, 77 Jefferson Avenue, Columbus, OH 43215; 614-464-1032. North Market, 59 Spruce Street, Columbus, OH 43215; 614-463-9664. Cosi, Ohio's Center Of Science & Industry (moving in November 1999 to west bank of Scioto River), Columbus, OH 43215; 614-228-COSI (228-2674). German Village Society, 588 South Third Street, Columbus, OH 43206; 614-221-8888. Columbus Museum of Art, 480 East Broad Street, Columbus, OH 43215; 614-221-6801. Short North, located on High Street, north of downtown, 614-421-1030. Columbus Santa Maria, 50 West Gay Street, Columbus, OH 43215; 614-645-8760. The Columbus Zoo, 9990 Riverside Drive, Powell, OH 43065; 614-645-3400. Franklin Park Conservatory and Botanical Garden, 1777 East Broad Street, Columbus, OH 43203-2040; 614-645-8733. Wexner Center for the Arts, The Ohio State University, 1871 North High Street, Columbus, OH 43210; 614-292-3535.

Central

31

Couples Only, Please!

LOOKING FOR A LITTLE SPARK TO HELP REKINDLE THE FIRE? Perhaps a hideaway in the Hocking Hills is just what the doctor ordered. For starters, book a back-to-nature weekend retreat. Send the kids to Grandma's house, pack your bags, and escape with your special someone. Here's a brief peek at some of the accommodations that the Hocking Hills area offers.

The Inn at Cedar Falls

Awaken to the sweet songs of chirping birds. The comfy quarters with the queen-size bed at The Inn at Cedar Falls will encourage the two of you to stay and cuddle the morning away. But, breakfast should not be missed. Follow the warm aroma of freshly brewed coffee drifting from the kitchen in the nearby log house. Wander inside and watch as a chef prepares a gourmet morning feast. Will it be French toast stuffed with orange marmalade and cream cheese? Or the German scramble—a combo of peppers, onions, potatoes, sausage, and eggs. Add a glass of juice, fresh fruit, and a homemade muffin. After breakfast, pour yourself another cup of coffee and mosey on out to the porch. Perhaps you'll spot a bluebird, yellow finch, or hummingbird.

On the hill behind the log house, an attractive barnlike structure offers cozy guest quarters. The rooms are decorated with a spattering of antiques, sans television and telephones. A platter of yummy "inn-made" oatmeal-raisin cookies awaits couples on check-in day. The common room supplies tea and coffee setups, reading material, and a wood-burning stove.

Log cabins are another overnight option. The Tree House, one of six cabins on the property, overlooks a forest of maple, pine, and oak trees. Walk out on the back deck and gaze down into the ravine. Be on the lookout for deer, raccoon, or an occasional wild turkey. Slim chance of finding this natural backdrop in the big city.

Glenlaurel

The woods and hidden pathways leading to Camusfearna Gorge provide hand-holding couples a rare opportunity to lounge on a blanket or linger over a picnic lunch. Guests at Glenlaurel, a Scottish-influenced hideaway, oftentimes seek out the spectacular gorge and surrounding countryside.

Meals are served in the Manor House. Soul mates can share an intimate dinner in an alcove in the Glasgow Dining Room. Couples wishing to mingle with other guests are invited to dine at the hewn table for ten in the Edinburgh Dining Room. After dinner, take a stroll and find your way back to your room. Turn on the muted lights, fill the double whirlpool tub, and get reacquainted with your partner.

In addition to private rooms in the Manor House, guests have an option of staying in the Cottages of Thistle Ridge. These very attractive cottages, a short walk from the main complex, supply the ultimate in seclusion. The dense forest, the open-air hot tub with private deck, a two-person shower, and a kitchenette guarantee a weekend of intimacy.

Ravenwood Castle

Working too many hours? Feeling frazzled? Perhaps a touch of medieval England will soothe the soul. Perched on a hilltop sits Ravenwood Castle encircled by acres of the Wayne National Forest. A drawbridge leads guests to the castle's front entrance. Rooms and suites are located in 12th-century-style towers.

Choose a king suite with second-floor parlor, a queen room, or a room with two double beds. The Great Hall, furnished with carved tables and chairs and large stained-glass windows from an old church, accommodates diners. Breakfast is always made "from scratch." Changing entrees include applesauce muffins, cinnamon rolls, ham-and-cheese quiche, and baked royal hash. Dinner is available at an extra charge.

Feeling creative? Ravenwood Castle offers getaway workshops for couples. Pick up some helpful hints on watercolor painting, or discover some tricks on how to write a children's book.

Sometime during your romantic weekend, plan to explore the surrounding spectacular parks. (See Chapter 32.) Or treat your partner to a train ride on the Hocking County Scenic Railroad in nearby Nelsonville.

Now, don't you both feel *lots* better?

141

FOR MORE INFORMATION

The Inn at Cedar Falls is open year-round except Christmas. Write to: The Inn at Cedar Falls, 21190 State Route 374, Logan, OH 43138, or call 800-65-FALLS (653-2557) or 614-385-7489. Glenlaurel is located at 15042 Mt. Olive Road, Rockbridge, OH 43149-9738. Call 800-809-REST (809-7378) or 740-385-4070. For information on Ravenwood Castle, write to 65666 Bethel Road, New Plymouth, OH 45654, or call 800-477-1541.

For information on all area attractions, contact the Hocking County Tourism Association, 13178 State Route 664 South, Logan, OH 43138; 800-HOCKING (462-5464) or 740-385-9706, or reach them at their website: www.hocking hills.com.

32

Hocking Hills:
A Four-Seasons Haven

BLAME IT ON THAT DARN WISCONSIN GLACIER.

A long, long time ago, huge bodies of ice plowed through the northern half of the Buckeye State, leaving behind massive twisted bedrock, deep gorges, and a wonderland of jagged cliffs.

"This is the beach to the lake that covered Ohio 100 million years ago," said Sam Wolfe, vice president, Hocking County Tourism Association. "The Wisconsin glacier pushed water out of the lake, the glacier started to melt, and eventually it eroded the sandstone. We still have erosion. The gorges are still forming."

Thanks to the glacier, the Hocking Hills area furnishes four seasons of spectacular hiking trails dotted with waterfalls, streams, and hidden caves.

Let's start with the coldest season to see what lures crowds to this region.

The third Saturday in January attracts throngs of hikers to Hocking Hills State Park for the annual Winter Hike. Participants ranging in shapes from the macho-muscular physique to the couch-potato bod gather in the park. Grab your earmuffs and mittens. Unpredictable January squalls oftentimes produce frigid, bone-chilling winds. Snowy pathways and ice-covered trails add to the challenge. Some years, the air feels almost balmy as the thermometer registers in the fifty-degree range.

The hike begins at the park's Old Man's Cave. The ranger-led six-mile trip weaves up, down, and through a winter paradise of natural-formed bedrock. Take a lunch break at Cedar Falls, the halfway marker. Bowls of bean soup, corn bread, and mugs of steamy cocoa are served. Too cold to continue? Legs tired? Not a problem. Vans transport hikers back to the starting line. Hardier souls trek the remaining three miles of trails from Cedar Falls to Ash Cave. In extreme cold, the ninety-foot waterfall at Ash Cave freezes, forming an awesome icicle mass. Bring your camera.

Depending on weather conditions, the hike averages four to five hours to complete. Pink-cheeked and glowing, hikers board buses and head back to the trail's starting point. Wonder what surprises Old Man Winter has in store for next year's hike.

As the weeks slowly pass, the park's personality shifts, shaking off the remains of the wicked winter. Streams swell, and patches of spring foliage appear on bare branches. Hiking trails bear a new look. Old Man's Cave, named after a hermit who supposedly lived in the cave after the Civil War, sports a slew of curious geological formations. Can you find the stately looking Sphinx head? Take a few minutes to stop at the Devil's Bathtub, a pothole formed in the sandstone of the valley floor. Listen to the deafening whirlpool of churning water.

In the summer months, families fill the state park's campground and cabins. There are no sleeping facilities at the seasonal lodge. However, you'll find a restaurant, a TV lounge, a game room, and an outdoor swimming pool.

Ash Cave, the largest and most impressive recess cave in the state, was so-named because of the mounds of ashes discovered on its floor. The horseshoe-shape cave measures seven hundred feet from end to end, with a rim rising ninety feet. Check out the mixed hues of green, red, and yellow bedrock as you hike the trails. Ash Cave is totally handicapped accessible.

Autumn shows off yet another face. Much of the lush green foliage begins to fade. This is a great season to journey approximately three miles south of Old Man's Cave to Cedar Falls, a steep-walled, hemlock-filled gorge. Another option—hike the shaded paths at Conkle's Hollow. Warning: Exercise extreme caution on the Rim Trail encircling this gorge.

Plan a prewinter picnic near Rock House, an opening in the face of the sandstone cliff along a series of cracks. Climb inside the "house of rock" for a better view of the effects of weathering on this area.

Cantwell Cliffs, in the northern reaches of Hocking Hills, offers trails surrounded by steep cliffs and deep woods. Can *you* slide through the passageway nicknamed "Fat Woman's Squeeze"?

No doubt about it—the Wisconsin glacier did a great job!

For More Information

The Hocking Hills area is approximately a one-hour drive southeast of Columbus. The six separate areas (Ash Cave, Old Man's Cave, Cedar Falls, Conkle's Hollow, Rock House, and Cantwell Cliffs) are known collectively as Hocking Hills State Park. Contact the Hocking Hills State Park, 20160 State Route 664, Logan, OH 43138-9537; 614-385-6841. For further information on all area attractions, contact the Hocking County Tourism Association, 13178 State Route 664 South, Logan, OH 43138, 800-HOCKING (462-5464) or 740-385-9706, or visit their website at www.hockinghills.com.

33

Caves, Castles, and Covered Bridges

LOGAN COUNTY

The Caves

THE AIR TEMPERATURE REGISTERS A REFRESHING FIFTY-TWO degrees as a handful of amateur spelunkers descend the steps into Zane Shawnee Caverns. We chuckle when we hear the story about the late-19th-century townspeople who entered the cave. It was quite a task. They were charged ten cents to be lowered via a wicker basket to get a glimpse of the inside of the "hole." Modern visitors find the descent much easier. Steps and ramps provide access to a depth of 132 feet below the ground.

Keenan, our fourteen-year-old guide, slowly leads us through the sometimes narrow passageways as an occasional droplet of water bounces off our shoulders and shoes. We appreciate his leisurely pace. As our journey continues, we stop several times to view rare cave pearls that are formed by a combination of iron and calcite, and then we marvel at the hollow soda-straw formations hanging from the ceiling. Before our expedition comes to an end, we pass by a solid cream-colored crystal measuring more than eight feet long. For many of us, this formation ranks as our favorite.

Zane Shawnee Caverns, east of the town of Bellefontaine (say: Bell-FOUN-ten), is a good starting point for a family weekend in Logan County. This picturesque west-central Ohio landscape renders a collection of caves, castles, and 19th-century covered bridges.

While you're still in the mood for cave exploring, check out Ohio Caverns, located on the outskirts of West Liberty and to the south of Bellefontaine. Year-round tours are offered. You'll discover rooms decorated with iridescent, icicle-like formations named stalactites (deposits that hang "tight" from the ceiling) and stalagmites (deposits that "might" reach the ceiling). The walls and ceilings of Ohio's largest cave disclose earthy shades of orange, red, and brown iron oxide. Look in the crevices for hints of mauve, blue, and gray concentrations. These muted deposits are the result of manganese dioxide.

"Touch it, pick it up, squeeze it," encourages our guide as he reaches for the only crystal that we are allowed to touch. This crystal is more than 10,000 years old. We make several more stops to admire the endless array of crystal formations that come in different sizes.

In the late 1800s, the first visitors to the cave missed most of the cavern's beauty. They were using small oil lanterns to see. Concrete walkways and a lighting system have been installed for 20th-century, one-hour tours.

Castles

Next stop: the houses of two extravagant brothers who decided to build their showy homes in the peaceful countryside that they enjoyed in their youth.

Drive north of Ohio Caverns on the two-lane country road and you'll find the original home of editor, poet, and farmer General Abram S. Piatt. As you enter Mac-A-Cheek

Castle (an Indian name meaning "smiling valley"), take note of the stained-glass windows on both sides of the entrance-way. A pair of 1800s Japanese porcelain umbrella stands adds to the lavish furnishings. Look up at the decorative, hand-painted roof garden scene in the Gothic-inspired drawing room. Stenciled vines and flowers are wrapped around the high ceiling edges. The chocolate-and-tan wood slat floors were constructed from materials found on the Piatts' land.

Abram's mammoth wooden front stairway signifies his status as an 1870s wealthy home owner. Upstairs, check out the general's eight-foot-high headboard with canopy. The sitting room, stocked with a collection of firearms and swords, reflects Abram's tastes.

Exits and entrances were numerous in the mansion. If you lived here, which one would you use—the servants' door-way, the carriage entry, the kitchen entrance, or the formal doorway?

As you leave Mac-A-Cheek Castle, turn left at the township road. Within minutes, you'll discover Pioneer House, a restored 1828 log cabin. This home belonged to Elizabeth and Benjamin Piatt, parents of the two brothers.

Wander around the rooms in search of a special collectible or craft. However, the real attraction at the cabin is the story connected with the upstairs bedroom behind the trapdoor. When the Piatt family lived here, slavery was a heated issue. Elizabeth was an abolitionist; her husband a federal judge. When Benjamin was not at home, Elizabeth led fugitive slaves through the attic to a concealed room on the other side of the house. The slaves were safe with Elizabeth.

When you leave Pioneer House, head for the home of Donn Piatt, a flamboyant writer, editor, and entertainer. Donn built Mac-O-Chee Castle about a mile down the road from his brother's mansion. The castle, completed in 1881, was planned as a retirement haven for his ailing wife, Louise. Unfortunately, Louise died of tuberculosis on the journey from Cincinnati to her new home.

Caves, Castles, and Covered Bridges

Tours of the thirty-seven-room mansion, decorated in walnut, pine, and oak, highlight the Piatt family's living space and servant areas. The drawing room, with hand-painted ceiling, served as the ladies' "gab" quarters. Men gathered in the library to enjoy brandy and cigars.

Peek inside the formal dining room, where nine-course meals were served. Notice the spice chest equipped with lock and key. Only the most dedicated servants were entrusted with the keys, as sugars and spices were expensive.

Before you depart, wander upstairs. The wide, elegant stairway to the second floor leads guests under a hand-painted "Pleasant Dreams" greeting on the ceiling. Ella, Donn's second wife, wished her overnight friends warm and pleasing thoughts as they ascended to their rooms on the third floor.

Central

Covered Bridges

After touring the magnificent castles, satisfy the covered-bridge enthusiasts in the group. Logan County boasts two 19th-century bridges. Both the Bickham Bridge (County Road 38 off State Route 366) and McColly Bridge (County Road 13, west off State Route 235) are easily accessible. A county map makes discovery of the two treasures an easy family task.

FOR MORE INFORMATION

Some of the attractions in Logan County are seasonal. Call or write for information before making travel plans.
Contacts: Zane Shawnee Caverns, 7092 State Route 540, Bellefontaine, OH 43311; 937-592-9592. Ohio Caverns, 2210 State Route 245 East, West Liberty, OH 43357; 937-465-

4017. Piatt Castles, 10051 Township Road 47, PO Box 497, West Liberty, OH 43357; 937-465-2821. Pioneer House, 10245 Township Road 47, PO Box 705, West Liberty, OH 43357; 937-465-4801. Or contact the Logan County Convention & Tourism Bureau, 100 South Main Street, Bellefontaine, OH 43311; (toll-free) 888-564-2626. Website www.logancountyohio.com\tourism.html.

Caves, Castles, and Covered Bridges

34

Marion Hot Spots

MY FAVORITE RAILROAD AFICIONADO INFORMS ME THAT "seventy trains pass through Marion each day." That's a hefty amount of train traffic. Screeches of metal thumping along the tracks near Union Station delight even non-railroad fans. The "in-the-process-of-restoration" train station, situated close to a series of tracks that permit rail travel in all four directions, attracts model railroaders. On weekends they gather in the former baggage building of the station. The public is invited to come inside and view the model train exhibit. (If you plan to visit during the week, call for an appointment.)

Train watching is a popular pastime in Marion, but it isn't the only game in town. Let's leave the railroad buffs at their "hot spot" and check out some of the other sites in the city.

- Visitors to the Harding Home and Museum are treated to a peek at the private life of the twenty-ninth president.

  On July 8, 1891, Florence King married Warren G. Harding. The wedding ceremony took place in the foyer of their newly built Elizabethan-style home on Mt. Vernon Avenue. The couple lived here until they left for Washington for the inauguration of Mr. Harding.

  "Eighty percent of everything in the home belonged to the Hardings," said Dick West, a local historian and volunteer for the Marion County Historical Society.

Visitors begin their tour of the house near the front porch, where Harding conducted his famous campaign speeches. Once inside, take note of the beautiful parquet floors in the parlor and a piano used by Mrs. Harding to teach piano lessons. She owned six pianos.

The wallpaper near the steps and covering the upstairs hall is the original 19th-century pattern. Glance inside the master bedroom. Mr. Harding's clothing hangs in the closet; personal items of Mrs. Harding are scattered neatly on the top of a dresser.

Take a walk outside to the adjacent building which West describes as "a very small and well-put-together museum."

This six-hundred-square-foot dwelling, a Sears Roebuck and Co. precut cottage, was erected for the working media, a place where they could "take a break." The museum now houses Harding memorabilia, including his golf clubs and numerous mementos of his achievements as president.

The Harding Home and Museum is open Wednesday through Sunday from Memorial Day through the last week of September. For a schedule of openings during the rest of the year, call the site.

Central

- The Harding Memorial, made of Georgian marble, was dedicated in 1931 by President Herbert Hoover. The impressive structure is the tomb of President and Mrs. Harding. The night-lights that surround the monument present a striking after-dark image. Viewing is available twenty-four hours a day.

- Hot peanuts! Hot popcorn! Step inside the circuslike setting (watch for the clowns!) at the Wyandot Popcorn Museum. Here you'll find the largest collection of poppers and peanut roasters in the world. Some of these antiquated machines still work—they can pop and butter corn.

Take your time as you stroll around. You'll discover quite an assortment of restored treasures: the original 1892 Olsen commercial dry popper; a 1927 Model T Cretors concession truck; and a horse-drawn Cretors Model D wagon with driver's seat.

The museum is located in Heritage Hall, which was once the site of the town's post office. Before you leave the stately complex, wander downstairs and peruse the collection of personal artifacts in the Harding Presidential Room.

- Carousel Concepts, a combination museum and workshop located on the outskirts of Marion, is one of the area's newest attractions. Enjoy a ride on a vintage carousel. Then watch a craftsman restore antique carousel pieces in the workshop area.

  Be sure to check out the room with the interesting telephone display. Telephone equipment dating from the days of Alexander Graham Bell, switchboards, and modern fiber optics are exhibited.

  The museum also features six-foot-high reproductions of Norman Rockwell's *Saturday Evening Post* covers.

- Marion celebrates an annual Popcorn Festival on the weekend after Labor Day. The three-day event, beginning on Thursday with a parade, features free entertainment from headliners such as the Pointer Sisters and REO Speedwagon. There's something for everyone—fine arts exhibits, crafts, beer gardens, and a Kiddie Korner.

- The historic late 1920s Palace Theatre presents live stage performances, movies, and concerts. Tours of this showplace, done in a Spanish courtyard motif, are available by appointment.

- Bring your golf clubs, weather permitting. The Marion area maintains five challenging courses. Inquire about lodging and golf packages at the visitor's bureau.

One final tidbit about Warren Harding before you leave town. The enterprising Mr. Harding, editor and owner of his own newspaper, began the tradition of home newspaper delivery.

FOR MORE INFORMATION

Central

For more information contact the Marion Area Convention & Visitors Bureau, 1952 Marion–Mt. Gilead Road, Marion, OH 43302; 800-371-6688. Or try their website: www.ma riononline.com.

Other contacts: Marion Union Station, 532 West Center Street, Marion, OH 43302; 740-383-3768. Harding Home and Museum, 380 Mt. Vernon Avenue, Marion, OH 43302; 740-387-9630. Harding Memorial, corner of Delaware Avenue and Vernon Heights Boulevard, Route 423, Marion. Wyandot Popcorn Museum, Heritage Hall, 169 East Church Street, Marion, OH 43302; 740-387-HALL (387-4255). Carousel Concepts, 2209 Marion Waldo Road, Marion, OH 43302; 740-389-9755. Palace Theatre, 276 West Center Street, Marion, OH 43302; 740-383-2101.

Southeast

35

Consider Cambridge

Mosser Glass

THE NEATLY LANDSCAPED, LITTLE RED HOUSE ON U.S. 22 caught our eye. We entered the front door and discovered a delightful parlorlike room. Shelves lined with various shapes, sizes, and colors of finished glass were displayed in showroom style. Closer inspection revealed water pitchers, butter dishes, bowls, and animal figurines—all manufactured by Mosser Glass. A tour of the factory behind the "house" was ready to begin.

Mindy, our guide, led the group through a side door to the stockroom and shipping area.

"There are two main ingredients in all glass—soda ash and silica sand," she said.

She pointed to the handmade cast-iron molds in the mold room, explained their use, and then led us to the rear of the building where sweltering heat from a fire-brick furnace permeated the area. We watched as the skilled factory workers removed pieces of molten glass from the two-thousand-degree oven.

"Glass needs to cool slowly," commented Mindy.

The workers placed the figurines on a conveyor belt for the three-and-a-half-hour cooling process.

Before our tour ended, we watched women carefully package the gorgeous glass products for shipping.

Quality glass manufacturing flourished during the early 1900s in Guernsey County, particularly in the city of Cambridge. Family-owned Mosser Glass continues the tradition. Smooth, cobalt-blue paperweights, cherry-red cardinals, and glass headlight lenses for antique cars are some of the company's specialties.

Regularly scheduled tours of the factory are given throughout the year, Monday through Friday, except for the first two weeks in July.

Living Word Outdoor Drama

The foothills of the Appalachian Mountains on the outskirts of Cambridge furnish an appropriate backdrop for outdoor drama.

What was once an eighty-acre farm now houses an amphitheater that seats 1,200 persons. A reenactment of the life, death, and resurrection of Jesus unfolds in this outside theater during the summer months. Roman arches, a temple made to scale, Pilate's marbleized court and residence, and a host of Jerusalem scenes stretch four hundred feet across the front of the stage.

As you sit in the audience during the moving performance, listen as Jesus delivers the Sermon on the Mount. Watch carefully as he celebrates the Passover meal with his disciples. You can almost feel his grief as he struggles to carry a cross up the hill to Calvary.

"We couldn't find a greater story that we'd like to tell," said Doris Snyder, general manager of the Living Word Outdoor Drama.

Tours of the set are given before performances.

Salt Fork Lodge Resort and Conference Center

Kids, couples, and grandparents alert! Salt Fork, the largest of the Ohio State Park lodges, delivers year-round recreation getaways that satisfy all ages. Surrounded by acres of wooded country, the lodge is located twenty minutes northeast of Cambridge.

Join the crowd at the HOOT-enanny, an after-dark search for owls. Perhaps a friendly game of family bingo is more to your liking. Teen Time and morning adult crafts are also provided. Swim any time of the year—the lodge has indoor and outdoor pools.

During the summer months, rent a fourteen-foot rowboat, a canoe, or a pontoon. A great relaxing way to see Salt Fork Lake is to reserve a seat on the sixty-five-passenger cruise boat. If golf is your game, book a tee time at the eighteen-hole championship course.

The resort offers special weekend discounts: Awaysis, New Year's Eve Package, Classic Halloween, and Sweetheart Weekend. Some packages include kids; others are geared for couples only. Reservations should be made well in advance.

Consider Cambridge

Other Cambridge-Area Attractions

- Take a free tour through a glass factory at Boyd's Crystal Art Glass. The factory and showroom are open Monday through Friday. During June, July, and August the showroom is also open Saturdays.

- Calling all shoppers! You'll find antiques, crafts, and collectibles at Penny Court. More than one hundred shops are located in this historic downtown district. Take a break from browsing at the 10th Street Antique Mall and visit the Hopalong Cassidy Museum. Free admission.

- The Cambridge Glass Museum houses a large display of Cambridge Art Pottery and more than five thousand pieces of Cambridge Glass. Call for hours of operation.

- Video programs and exhibits on the history of glassmaking in Cambridge and the Ohio Valley can be viewed at Degenhart Paperweight & Glass Museum. Admission charged.

For More Information

For further information, contact Mosser Glass, Inc., 9279 Cadiz Road (U.S. 22), Cambridge, OH 43725; 740-439-1827. The Living Word, 6010 College Hill Road, PO Box 1481, Cambridge, OH 43725; 740-439-2761. Salt Fork, Route 22 East, PO Box 7, Cambridge, OH 43725; 800-AT-A-PARK (282-7275) or 740-439-2751. Boyd's Crystal Art Glass, 1203 Morton Avenue, PO Box 127, Cambridge, OH 43725; 740-439-2077. Penny Court, 637 Wheeling Avenue, Cambridge, OH 43725; 740-432-4369. 10th Street Antique Mall, 127 South 10th Street, Cambridge, OH 43725; 740-432-3364. The Cambridge Glass Museum, 812 Jefferson Avenue, Cambridge, OH 43725; 740-432-3045. Degenhart Paperweight & Glass Museum, PO Box 186, Cambridge, OH 43725 (located at Highland Hill Road at U.S. 22 and I-77); 740-432-2626.

For all area attractions, contact the Cambridge/Guernsey County Visitors & Convention Bureau, 2250 Southgate Parkway, PO Box 427, Cambridge, OH 43725; 800-933-5480 or 740-432-2022. Website: www.cambridgeoh.com\guernsey countyinfo\.

36

Baskets Galore!

DRESDEN

BASKETS ARE A *REALLY* BIG DEAL IN DRESDEN.

For starters, the village park on the corner of Fifth and Main Streets is home to the world's "largest" basket. Check it out. The basket towers twenty-three feet from ground to the handles. It's constructed of handwoven hardwood maple trees and measures forty-eight feet long and eleven feet wide. Let the kids stand next to this oversize picnic basket, and be ready with your camera. It's a great photo opportunity!

Serious basket collectors and casual browsers stroll the downtown sidewalks. Perhaps your picnic basket needs a new checkered lining, or Aunt Suzie wants a frilly cover for her breadbasket. Looking for primitive folk art or birdhouses? Main Street shops stock every imaginable basket-related accessory as well as country crafts and collectibles. Basket lids and quilted liners decorated with happy pumpkin faces, oak wooden lids and dividers, basket tie-ons, and hand-carved items cram the store's shelves.

After your shopping spree, visit the downtown Longaberger Make A Basket Shop. Look for the navy blue awning draped above a small storefront building. Step inside. Here's a place where visitors are invited to learn how to make a Longaberger basket. Be sure to preregister to reserve a weaving time (740-754-6327).

Why the basket craze? The story emerges in the early 20th century when handwoven baskets were made by the Longaberger family, residents of the Dresden community. In 1973 the Longaberger Company employed five basket weavers. Today the multimillion-dollar industry employs more than 4,700 people to meet the demand for handmade baskets and a line of pottery.

Longaberger offers free tours of its Manufacturing Campus, located just west of Dresden. If you want to see the entire production process, plan to be at the complex before 1 P.M., Monday through Friday. When visitors arrive, they are encouraged to spend a few minutes in the Gallery, a room dedicated to past and present Longaberger products. Next, a forty-five-minute free tour begins on the mezzanine. Get ready for a leisurely stroll to watch the behind-the-scenes basket process. As visitors are led through the door to an observation walkway, the pleasant scent of wood stain filters through the air.

Groups are directed along the platform, stopping at seven different workstations. At one point, visitors watch as a weaver expertly maneuvers her fingers around and through the moist, pliable maple wood. Completion of Longaberger's twelve- to sixteen-week course at the School of Weaving is required for a person to qualify as a weaver. The size, shape, and difficulty of the basket determine a weaver's salary. When a basket is finished, using the centuries-old method, it is signed and dated. The baskets are made entirely by hand, without the use of glue or staples. Note the white tape wrapped around workers' fingers. The wet wood can easily cut the skin.

"How do the baskets get to be different colors?" asks a young visitor.

"The weaving material is dyed with Rit," answers the tour guide.

The Staining Chamber, producing six hundred gallons of water-based stain per day, reminds the onlookers of a miniature car wash. From their vantage point, they can see the outside of the Swing Chamber where the drying process begins.

As the tour draws to a close, watch as handles and lids are added to baskets; inspectors make repairs; leather straps are tied to a laundry basket to help keep the shape; and baskets are packed individually for shipping. The plant produces 30,000 to 35,000 baskets per day.

At the end of the tour is the Just For Fun Shop. Here visitors can purchase basket goodies, including the Dresden Tour Basket. All other Longaberger baskets are for sale via home demonstration parties.

FOR MORE INFORMATION

For more information contact the Dresden Village Association, PO Box 707, Dresden, OH 43821; 740-754-3401. Website: www.dresden-ohio.com. Or contact The Longaberger Company, Guest Relations, 740-754-6330. For information on all area attractions, contact the Zanesville–Muskingum County Convention & Visitors Bureau, 205 North Fifth Street, Zanesville, OH 43701; 800-743-2303 or 740-454-8687. Website: www.zanesville-ohio.com.

Baskets Galore!

37

Down on the Farm!

GALLIPOLIS

DURING THE SECOND FULL WEEKEND OF OCTOBER, THE BOB Evans Farm celebrates autumn. The atmosphere erupts with the sounds and sights of a down-on-the-farm festival near the Buckeye State's southern border.

Park your car and then meander around the spacious grounds. Stop and watch some old-fashioned demonstrations of how cows were milked, sheep were sheared, and horses were shod. Listen to the hog-calling contest. Or grab a partner and join in the feed-sack races.

More than 150 craftspeople demonstrate and sell a variety of American crafts made with outdated tools. You'll find storytellers, lumberjack shows, and horseshoe pitching. Entertainment abounds with the musical notes of country, bluegrass, jazz, and gospel.

Don't leave the fest without sampling some food. Homemade pies, ice cream, apple dumplings, and sausage sandwiches satisfy the hungry crowds.

Can't make the festival? Not to worry. The farm is open daily from Memorial Day weekend through Labor Day and the weekends in September. The 1,100-acre farm, located in Rio Grande (say: RYE-O GRAND), sports a long list of activities geared for families, couples, and singles alike.

Perhaps a laid-back canoe ride down a river through southeastern Ohio's wooded hillsides sounds appealing.

Then, sign up at the farm's canoe livery for an eleven-mile overnight excursion along the winding Raccoon Creek. If you enjoy horseback riding, reserve a spot on the Paddle & Saddle overnight trip offered by the livery and the riding stable.

Bring your tent or camper to the Bob Evans Farm Campground. Camping is available during regular farm hours of operation and also during April, May, and October, upon request.

Bob Evans started his restaurant business by serving his homemade sausage at a twelve-stool diner he owned in the nearby town of Gallipolis (say: GAL-a-po-LEES). As the popularity of his sausage grew, he eventually opened a little sausage shop on his farm. The Sausage Shop is now a Bob Evans Restaurant.

More Gallia County

- A scenic driving tour through the Gallia County region renders a great overview of the area. The forty-five-minute audio tour meanders through small communities, passes by country homes, and travels by farmlands. The cassette is set up so that the listener can begin and end at any point along the tour. You'll see old cemeteries; Fortification Hill, an ideal spot for cannon placement during the Civil War; historical homes; Rio Grande College; and an 1835 mill that once flourished along Raccoon Creek.

- Tour guides of Our House State Memorial in Gallipolis prefer the first-person role as they lead visitors through the circa-1819 tavern. Our House is typical of the taverns that doubled as inns during the 1800s.

  "We sleep eight to ten comfortably, and any number in semicomfort. You can sleep nose to toes," said the straight-faced guide, decked in her 19th-century garb.

She further explained: "Seventy-five cents for a bed; thirty cents for the floor."

As you stroll through the brick Federal-style building, note the formal dining room. The table is set for dessert with French porcelain dishes. Will the proprietor offer fruit, nuts, or custard pudding to his dinner guests?

Women were not allowed in the public dining room—unless they were serving food. Gentlemen were required to "mind their manners" and told "don't spit on the floor." If a man got too drunk, he was escorted to the basement to "sleep it off."

The ladies, dressed in their hoop skirts and bonnets, congregated in the drawing room. They would play a game, rock their babies, and sleep here.

Before you depart this nostalgic gathering spot, walk upstairs and check out the attic. You'll learn interesting trivia about some of the invited guests, including Revolutionary War hero the Marquis de Lafayette.

- The arts are alive and thriving in "the Old French City" of Gallipolis.

    Ariel Theatre, a cultural and performing arts center, is home to the only professional orchestra in southeast Ohio, the Ohio Valley Symphony. The acoustics, Victorian-style seats, and extensive stenciling provide the backdrop for first-class music, dance, and theater performances. Guided tours of the century-old treasure may be arranged.

    A regional multi-arts center, dubbed The French Art Colony, hosts numerous arts exhibits, music recitals, theatrical productions, and workshops. Historic "Riverby," a Federal-style brick home surrounded by a wrought-iron fence, is the center for these activities. Tours of the house

Down on the Farm!

and grounds, guided or on your own, are available during
gallery hours.

For More Information

For information on the audio driving tour and all area attrac-
tions, contact the Ohio Valley Visitors Center, 45 State
Street, Gallipolis, OH 45631; 800-765-6482 or 740-446-6882.
Website: eurekanet.com/~ovvc.

Other contacts: The Bob Evans Farm, PO Box 198, Rio
Grande, OH 45674; 800-994-FARM (994-3276) or 740-245-
5305. Our House State Memorial, 432 First Avenue, Gallipolis, OH, 45631; 740-446-0586. Morris and Dorothy
Haskins Ariel Theatre, 426 Second Avenue, Gallipolis, OH
45631; 740-446-ARTS (446-2787). The French Art Colony,
530 First Avenue, PO Box 472, Gallipolis, OH 45631; 740-
446-3834.

38

Are You a Skidder?

THE ANNUAL BLACK WALNUT FESTIVAL IN MONROE COUNTY features demonstrations and competitions of modern machines used for harvesting timber. Participants simulate the job skills of the timber industry in an arena. Kids walk around the fairgrounds covering their ears with their hands, as saws buzz and antique engines and tractors rev up.

Bill Bolton judges knuckleboom loader contests at the festival. The knuckleboom loader machine, used in the timber industry to pile logs or load logs onto a truck, is similar to a large backhoe with a "hand" on the end of it. The operator sits in the cab or on a truck-mount and controls the machine by maneuvering a lever.

Of course, Bolton wouldn't be able to be a judge unless he knew a whole lot about the twelve-ton machines.

"I regularly compete," he said.

Bolton explains the competition: "Four logs, approximately twelve feet long and fourteen to fifteen inches in diameter, are placed in a staggered line. The knuckleboom operator grasps the logs, places them in a metal bunk, and then puts them back in the original chalk lines."

What's a judge looking for?

"Eye-hand coordination with the machine," said Bolton, who is a spokesperson for Native Manufacturing, Inc.

Contestants are judged on speed and precision in placing the logs. The entire process takes about one and a half minutes. The winner receives a cash prize.

"When you buy a two-by-four, you don't know what happens from the tree to the store. This is a way we can show people what we do. People come to watch because it's a job that a lot of people don't see; they are curious to see what goes on and what it takes," explains Bolton.

If you go to the fest, be sure to watch an "all-around woodsman." He throws an ax at the bull's-eye, operates a noisy crosscut saw, and expertly chops wood.

So—how's your "nail-driving" technique? If you can drive a nail without bending it, or pound one hundred nails in a matter of seconds, sign up for the Nail Driving Contest.

Are you a skidder? Most city folks aren't. But if you happen to possess the skills, try the Skidder Competition. The twelve-ton skidder, the ultimate four-wheeler, is used when the timber is harvested. It's "the working horse—it physically brings the timber out of the forest."

During the festival competition, cones are set up in a curved configuration on a large grassy course. Walnuts are placed on top of the cones. The skidder operator's job is to follow all safety steps while dragging the cable from the skidder to the nearby log, manually looping the log, checking safety belts, and then dragging the twenty-foot log through the obstacle course. Whew! If walnuts are knocked off the cones, points are taken away. The contestant is judged on speed, skill, and safety. Total time: less than two minutes.

Hungry from watching all the activity? Then, wander off to the food booths for a taste of black-walnut-flavored recipes. Sample the scrumptious black-walnut pies, muffins, and ice cream. Or savor the open-kettle homemade apple butter.

Carnival rides are absent from the festival grounds but not missed. Banjo music, foot-stomping fiddle players, and square dancing keep the crowds happily entertained. Kids enjoy wagon rides, trips to the petting zoo, and face painting.

If you're interested in black walnuts, Bolton suggests that you explore further: "There are a good bit of black walnut trees around. In the fall, when walnuts mature, they're the size of a tennis ball, with a green covering on the top of the nut. Take the covering off and find the walnut inside."

For More Information

The Black Walnut Festival is held the second full weekend in October at the Monroe County Fairgrounds, State Route 26, Woodsfield. Admission is charged to the grounds. For further information contact the Black Walnut Festival, PO Box 643, Woodsfield, OH 43793-0643; 740-472-5499. For information on all attractions in the Monroe County area, contact the Monroe County Chamber of Commerce, PO Box 643, Woodsfield, OH 43793-0643; 740-472-5499.

173

Are You a Skidder?

39

A Riverboat Town

MARIETTA

RIVER-STYLE TRAFFIC JAMS ARE RARE IN MARIETTA, WITH THE exception of the weekend after Labor Day. That's when "Ohio's first city" celebrates a final summer surge. Pleasure boats arrive by the hundreds. Dozens of riverboats crowd the banks. The parade of boats presents a colorful spectacle as the annual Ohio River Sternwheel Festival kicks into high gear.

On the Saturday during the fest, fireworks burst into sparkling specks of color to the delight of the blanket crowd. Dancers, singers, and musicians entertain festivalgoers. On the final day of the bash, pick your favorite stern-wheeler and cheer as the race begins. Who will finish first?

This riverboat town, which borders the banks of the Ohio and Muskingum Rivers, shares more than boat races. Let's amble through the streets of Marietta and see what's happening.

- Pioneer Rufus Putnam constructed his home on a small hill near present-day Washington Street. This land was called Campus Martius, the site of a civilian fortification built to protect Marietta from the enemy. A spectacular view of the confluence of the two rivers was once visible from this vantage point.

Putnam's home, now cleverly enclosed within a museum complex, stands on the original 18th-century site. "Campus Martius: The Museum of the Northwest Territory," showcases the development of Marietta, the first organized American settlement in the Northwest Territory. Close your eyes as you stand in the doorway of Putnam's circa-1700s poplar wood house. Try to imagine how it felt to live in fear of Indian raids. Fortunately, Indians never attacked this civilian fort.

Stroll through the rooms of the Putnam house. Note the rope beds with straw tick mattresses and canopies to keep dust and bugs out. Three upstairs bedrooms (a rare feature during this time period) are proof of Putnam's elite status. Putnam held the position of superintendent of the land company responsible for Marietta's settlement.

The large museum also houses the Ohio Company Land Office, a historic structure where some of the earliest maps of the Northwest Territory were made. Don't leave the complex without perusing the displays of tools, furnishings, and artifacts that relate to the founding of this region. Plan to spend several hours here.

• Next stop, the Ohio River Museum. In the 18th and 19th centuries the flatboat provided the major method of transportation for settlers traveling west into Ohio. Take the kids and climb aboard a replicated flatboat on the grounds of the museum. The boat, dismantled when it reached its destination, was used to build the settler's house.

The last surviving steam towboat in America, the *W. P. Synder Jr.*, is permanently moored on the river outside the museum. Visitors are invited to walk aboard this circa-1918 boat.

What's a snagboat? Did the *Delta Queen* serve a specific purpose? You'll discover the answers to these questions as you meander around the museum exhibits. Artifacts, a life-size diorama, and a multimedia show provide insight into the days of riverboat transportation. The museum consists of three exhibit buildings that are connected by covered walkways. The museum is closed December through February.

- Looking for a laid-back view of the riverboat town? Book a passage on the *Valley Gem*, a three-hundred-passenger stern-wheeler. A dinner cruise along the Muskingum and Ohio Rivers provides a relaxed evening adventure for the entire family.

  The stern-wheeler operates April through September. Weekend foliage tours are offered during October.

- Ever taste red cabbage beet linguine? How does flavored gourmet lasagna sound? Pastas not of the usual grocery-store variety await shoppers at Rossi Pasta. As you open the front door of the downtown shop, breathe deeply. A tantalizing aroma of basil, oregano, and garlic gradually fills your nostrils. See freshly made pasta hung to dry. Pick up a free sample. There are no regularly scheduled tours; however, staff members are happy to answer pasta-making questions.

- "Boo" the villain; "cheer" the hero. Audience participation is encouraged as the melodrama unfolds at the permanently moored *Showboat Becky Thatcher* Theater. The historic riverboat also features a restaurant and lounge.

- Take a walk across the pedestrian bridge that links downtown Marietta with historic Harmar Village. A handful of shopping possibilities awaits browsers. Check out the Children's Toy and Doll Museum, housed in a restored B&O railroad car, and then take a peek at the extensive display of Coca-Cola memorabilia at Butch's Cola Museum.

A Riverboat Town

- Before you leave this corner of the state, plan a side trip. Just follow the Ohio River in a southwest direction from Marietta to the town of Belpre. Here you'll discover the Lee Middleton Original Doll Factory on Washington Boulevard. Arrange to join the free guided tour, and watch the factory workers mold, hand-paint, and assemble porcelain and vinyl dolls. Shoppers in the group should be sure to browse the attached factory outlet store.

FOR MORE INFORMATION

For further information on all area attractions, contact the Marietta/Washington County Convention & Visitors Bureau, 316 Third Street, Marietta, OH 45750; 800-288-2577 or 740-373-5178. Website: www.rivertowns.org.

Other area contacts: Campus Martius: The Museum of the Northwest Territory, 601 Second Street, Marietta, OH 45750; 800-860-0145 or 740-373-3750. Ohio River Museum, 601 Front Street, Marietta, OH 45750; 800-860-0145 or 740-373-3750. *Valley Gem* Stern-Wheeler, 123 Strecker Hill, Marietta, OH 45750; 740-373-7862. Rossi Pasta, 114 Greene Street, Marietta, OH 45750; 800-227-6744 or 740-376-2065. *Showboat Becky Thatcher*, 237 Front Street, Marietta, OH 45750; 740-373-6033 (theater) or 740-373-4130 (restaurant). Children's Toy and Doll Museum, 206 Gilman Street, Marietta, OH 45750; 740-373-4121. Butch's Cola Museum, 118 Maple Street, Marietta, OH 45750; 740-376-COKE (376-2653); Lee Middleton Original Doll Factory, 1301 Washington Boulevard, Belpre, OH 45714; 800-233-7479 or 740-423-1481.

Southeast

40

Canoe Country and More

MONROE COUNTY

BEAVERS AND RIVER OTTERS HANG OUT IN THE LITTLE
Muskingum River. If you're very quiet (and a little lucky),
you might see one of the critters from your canoe. There
are thirty-five miles of waters on the Little Muskingum that
are suitable for canoeing. You'll find canoe launches scattered
along the river's edge. On lazy summer afternoons, canoers
paddle to the shore and break for a picnic lunch. Here in
Ohio's southeastern hills, outdoor lovers thrive on endless
recreation choices.

Not really interested in paddling a canoe? Then why not
check out some of the region's other treasures? Here's a look
at what's happening on Ohio's southeastern turf:

- The banks surrounding the Little Muskingum River provide camping, hiking trails, fishing, and hunting opportunities. Campers will discover primitive campgrounds
with picnic tables, grills, and fire rings. Clearly marked
trails supply hikers with back-to-nature escapes.

- Fishing opportunities abound in Monroe County, an area
affectionately dubbed the "Switzerland of Ohio." Populations of small- and largemouth bass, rock bass, perch,
muskie, and catfish live in one of the "purest streams in

Ohio," the Little Muskingum. Fishing licenses and rental equipment are available.

- Meander through any of the four covered bridges that cross the river. Of special interest is the Knowlton Covered Bridge, the second-longest covered bridge in Ohio, measuring 195 feet. An excellent brochure, published by the Wayne National Forest office, leads travelers on a self-guided tour of the bridges, a circa-1890s general store, and several old barn paintings advertising Mail Pouch Tobacco.

- Piatt Park (east of the town of Woodsfield), sprinkled with rare white trillium and various species of flora and fauna, attracts family picnickers and hikers. Be forewarned: Steep hills and lots of steps carve a path to the park's natural cave. For the camping crowd, water and electrical hookups are available in the 119-acre park.

- Enjoy a ride on the *Fly Ferry*, a tourist's stern-wheeler transportation link for vehicles between Ohio and West Virginia. Or stand on the overlook at Hannibal Locks and Dam, a modern navigational dam on the Ohio River.

- The Wayne National Forest, located in twelve of Ohio's southeast counties, has been used and inhabited continuously for twelve thousand years. The forest's span of activity began when mastodons roamed the land. Traders and adventure seekers settled here in the 1700s. In later years, lumber, oil, coal mining, and iron smelting provided profits for the settlers.

  Modern-day visitors hunt and fish in the vast forest. Off-road-vehicle areas, horse trails, and water-access sites for swimming and boating entice travelers to the hills' natural beauty.

After spending some leisure hours in the Buckeye State's southeastern corner, it's easy to see why two of the local byways, Routes 26 and 78, have received recognition as being among the "ten top driver roads in the country."

For More Information

For information on area attractions, contact the Wayne National Forest, 219 Columbus Road, Athens, OH 45701; 740-592-6644. Or contact the Monroe County Chamber of Commerce, PO Box 643, Woodsfield, OH 43793-0643; 740-472-5499. For Piatt Park info, contact the Monroe County Park Board, Courthouse, Third Floor, 101 North Main Street, Woodsfield, OH 43793, 740-472-1328. To obtain a copy of the Covered Bridge Scenic Byway Auto Tour brochure, contact the Marietta Unit, Forest Service, Rural Route 1, Box 132, Marietta, OH 45750; 740-373-9055.

Canoe Country and More

41

Floodwall Art

PORTSMOUTH

Dusk descends on the riverside town of Portsmouth.
An iridescent blue early-evening sky outlines the hustle and bustle
of downtown Chillicothe Street. Fat-fender cars hover dangerously
close to the ground, sidewalk lamps illuminate the storefronts, and
clusters of window-shoppers linger.

Jonathan, my teenage travel partner, saunters up to a lit lamp-
post and leans his palm against the aqua-colored fixture. He grins,
poses for the camera, and then continues his walk.

Except for the young man, this entire 1940s scene is a
mural painting on a floodwall.

Yes, a floodwall.

The movie-screen-size mural appears so lifelike that the
developed photo of Jonathan gives the illusion that he is
actually standing on Chillicothe Street.

Floodwalls serve a very obvious purpose for this southern
Ohio city. Yet, muralist Robert Dafford has managed to
transform the drab concrete walls of Portsmouth into a
vibrant outdoor art gallery.

The murals, most of them measuring forty feet in length
and twenty feet high, tell stories about the people and
events of the area, spanning a period from prehistoric times
to the present.

Sports fans, do you remember the legendary Jim Thorpe?
In 1927 Thorpe was a player and coach for the Portsmouth

Shoe Steels. A larger-than-life painting of Thorpe in his dark brown football jersey and tan pants, a detailed team photo, and an "action" shot of Thorpe playing ball present a glimpse of the athlete's life.

In another scene, painted in crisp blues and winter whites, the artist depicts Native Americans in an early-1700s snow-covered Shawnee village.

The murals represent a wide and varied range of topics: slow-moving canal traffic along the Ohio and Erie Canal (circa late 1800s); 19th-century farmers harvesting wheat from the fertile Ohio Valley; and the lovely Julia Marlowe, world-renowned Shakespearean actress.

Touchdown! Football surfaces once again on a wall as artist Dafford replays the famous "Iron Man" game of 1932. A referee, clad in knickers and sporting a black bow tie, extends his arms straight up in the air. Frustrated Packer players wrap their arms around the unstoppable Spartans, but to no avail. The Portsmouth Spartans beat the Green Bay Packers by a score of 19 to 0.

Dafford's two thousand feet of art demonstrate his spectacular talent for attention to detail. Crisp, clearly defined paintings add spark to the once ordinary Ohio River floodwalls protecting Front Street.

Take your pick: walk, jog, or bike past the murals. Or stay in your car and slowly creep along the road. You'll probably want to get out and take a closer look at what Jonathan describes as "awesome."

Other Attractions

- Visit the "1810 House" on Waller Street, a museum that depicts pioneer living. It's located just minutes by car from the floodwalls. Look for the side door with a short rope hanging from the latchkey entrance. A gentle pull magically opens the door. Wander throughout the stately four-room home owned by the Kinney family and discover a potpourri of artifacts dating from the early 1800s through the mid-20th century.

The museum staff encourages a "hands-on" policy. It's OK to touch the Paul Revere lantern, play a few bars on the century-plus organ, or gently rub the dark burgundy and forest green wedding dresses worn by brides in the 1800s. Before leaving the museum, check out the petticoat table. The low-to-the-floor mirror probably hung at the bottom of a stairway in order that ladies could check to see if their slips were showing. Tours are by appointment. Call 740-353-2099.

- Next, venture over to the post-office building. A small one-room exhibit in the basement houses a collection of Roy Rogers memorabilia. Record albums, books, cowboy boots, and toys fill the display cases. Call 740-353-0900 to make an appointment.

  Roy Rogers fans meet annually during the first weekend in June at the downtown Ramada Inn. Look-alike contests, "Breakfast with the Stars," and a slew of cowboy/cowgirl and Western paraphernalia highlight the Roy Rogers Festival.

- Twenty miles east of Portsmouth in the town of Franklin Furnace, you can book a leisurely cruise on the *Buckeye Belle*. The three-hour Ohio River trip begins with a passage through a lock chamber. Call 800-671-0055 for times of departure.

- The annual River Days Festival is held on Labor Day weekend. You'll find arts and crafts, food booths, and an assortment of entertainment. Call 740-353-7647 for specific times.

Floodwall Art

- The Old Fashioned Sorghum Makin' celebration takes place on John Simon's Farm, approximately fifteen minutes from downtown Portsmouth. If you're interested in old-time music, apple-butter making, and horse-and-buggy rides, make plans to attend this annual October fest. Call 740-259-6337 for more details.

For More Information

To find the floodwall murals, follow the green "Murals" signs that are posted on Washington Street (State Route 23 South). For detailed information on all area attractions, contact the Portsmouth Convention & Visitors Bureau, 324 Chillicothe Street, Portsmouth, OH 45662; 740-353-1116.

Southeast

42

Hideaway in the Foothills

SHAWNEE STATE PARK RESORT

LUNCHTIME WINDS DOWN AS THE LAST OF THE DINERS GAZE through the spacious glass windows overlooking the grounds. A fluttering, slender-billed hummingbird stops in midair just shy of the bird feeder. The bathing-suit-clad crowd slip into and out of the pool, a sure cure for the scorching summer steam. In the tree-filled hilly horizon, a small chunk of Turkey Creek Lake emerges. Mealtimes at Shawnee Lodge restaurant feature more than food.

Comfortably concealed in the Appalachian foothills, the Shawnee Resort and Conference Center attracts a mixed populace of family vacationers, singles, and couples.

Boredom is out of the question. Try a turtle race, squirt gun battle, balloon toss, family bingo, or putt-putt competition. Keep "all you find" at the penny dive at the indoor pool. Win a prize if you place first or second in the scavenger hunt.

"Yakety Yak, Let's Make Some Gak!" reads the Tuesday A.M. activity schedule. Kids gather in the lower lobby and listen as the activities director describes the secret "Gak" recipe. Hint: Common household products are used.

Not really interested in Gak? Then, gather the family together for the greased-watermelon frolic in the indoor pool. Melon slices served after the game.

Searching for a subdued and quieter sport? Join the group in the whirlpool, sauna, or exercise room. Or bring your golf clubs and play the eighteen-hole championship course overlooking the Ohio River. Boaters have access to the park's marina facility.

"Let's go wiking around the lake!"

Huh?

"Wiking," explains the state park naturalist, leading the hikers in the direction of Turkey Creek Lake, "is a combination of wading and hiking."

If "dry" adventures suit you better, join the nature hike, roast marshmallows, or attend an outdoor art class. Interested in a close encounter with some insects? Meet at the nature center.

Special "hands-on" outdoor excursions and activities for the seven- to fourteen-year-old gang help instill a deeper appreciation for the land, which once served as the hunting grounds for Shawnee Indians. A naturalist is on duty between Memorial Day and Labor Day.

There are no scheduled state park activities during the cold weather months, but that's OK. Winters provide a slew of outdoor opportunities. Bundle up. Explore the snow-covered hiking paths along a mile-long trail, or follow the animal tracks. Cross-country skiers glide across the park's hills. Perhaps ice fishing on Roosevelt or Turkey Creek Lake sounds appealing.

Back at the lodge, warm your insides with a mug of hot chocolate. Sit back and relax. Or check out the handcrafted cedar furnishings and Native American decorations scattered throughout the lobby.

Nearby Attractions

- The Shawnee State Forest encircles the state park and lodge. The forest, often referred to as "the Little Smokies of Ohio," is the largest of Ohio's state parks. More than seventy miles of bridle trails, numerous campsites, hunting, and fishing possibilities are available in the forest.

- Serpent Mound State Memorial (forty-five minutes northwest), one of the few effigies in Ohio, resembles a gigantic snake uncoiling in seven deep curves. Walk the grounds or visit the museum.

- The city of Portsmouth (Chapter 41), located on the Ohio River, is approximately fifteen minutes from the resort. Visit the floodwall murals or museums, or attend the annual Roy Rogers Festival.

FOR MORE INFORMATION

Shawnee Resort is one of eight Ohio State Park Resorts. The park is administered by the Ohio Division of Parks and Recreation. For park information contact Shawnee State Park, Star Route 68, Portsmouth, OH 45662; 740-858-6652.

For resort information contact the Shawnee Resort and Conference Center, State Route 125, PO Box 189, Friendship, OH 45630; 800-AT-A-PARK (282-7275) or 740-858-6621. Website: www.amfac.com.

For information on Shawnee State Forest, contact the Shawnee State Forest, 13291 U.S. 52, Portsmouth, OH 45663; 740-858-6685.

For Serpent Mound information, contact the Serpent Mound State Memorial, 3850 State Route 73, Peebles, OH 45660; 937-587-2796.

For information on all area attractions, contact the Portsmouth Convention & Visitors Bureau, 324 Chillicothe Street, Portsmouth, OH 45662; 740-353-1116.

Hideaway in the Foothills

43

Tecumseh!

The Backstage Tour

"WHY DON'T YOU JUST USE KETCHUP?" ASKS THE NINE-YEAR-old boy.

"Well, it's too expensive, the consistency is wrong, and it stains," replies Judith, our tour guide, referring to the thick red solution in her hand.

She holds the "body blood bag" high in the air so everyone can get a closer look. (Yucks and groans.) The bag, filled with a mixture of cornstarch, liquid Tide detergent, and red dye, is ready for tonight's outdoor theater performance.

"The *tasty* blood bag," explains Judith, "an odor-free mix of Karo syrup, red dye, and a hint of mint or cherry, is used in the mouth. Actors choose their favorite flavor." (More yucks and groans!)

Here we are, on the outskirts of Chillicothe on a backstage tour in the dense forest of Sugarloaf Mountain. What a fascinating peek at the behind-the-scenes activities. We learn that tonight's performance of *Tecumseh!* is a reenactment of the story of a great Shawnee leader. The show involves considerable combat and use of fire. No live fires, our guide tells us—only gas ones.

We stand on the dirt stage and peer out over the empty seats of the tiered amphitheater, looking upward to the production stage tower. That's the place where engineers over-see the sound and lighting instruments.

Adam, who portrays an Indian in the play, joins our group. BANG! He pulls the trigger on a replicated Kentucky rifle, demonstrating the blasts that the audience will hear.

Stuntman J.J. appears from backstage and wrestles Adam to the ground in a "bad-guy-versus-good-guy" mock fight. J.J. then scurries up the rocks onstage right and tumbles headfirst over a cliff. Lucky for J.J., a bed of hidden cushions breaks his fall.

"If you totally relax, you won't hurt yourself," he says, confidently.

We slowly climb the wooded path that parallels the theater seats. At the top of the slight hill are three working canons, modeled after 1812 English naval guns. The show's script calls for loud, thundering gunfire from these canons.

We conclude our tour near the bleachers in the rear of the complex.

"Any questions?" says our guide.

"What's your part in the play?" asks an elderly gentleman.

"I help 'woman' the canons," Judith replies.

Tours are given in the afternoon on performance days. They last approximately one hour.

The Play

The year is 1784. The still, summer evening explodes with howling, screeching voices. A bloody skirmish near the banks of the Ohio River takes place before the hushed crowd. Frontiersmen, caught in an ambush set by the Shawnee Indians, scurry frantically out of sight.

As the powerful tale unfolds, galloping horses appear from behind the trees, tomahawks zip across the stage, and a canoe skims the surface of the man-made pond in the background. The audience senses Tecumseh's pain and frustration. The young Shawnee leader longs for peace. He simply wants the land that was taken away returned to his people.

The story, filled with vengeance, violence, love, and deceit, is an appropriate family affair, except for very young children. All seats are reserved. Advance reservations are strongly recommended, particularly for weekends.

Other Area Attractions

- The Hopewell Culture National Historical Park preserves an ancient village and burial site for people who lived along the Scioto River during the first two centuries A.D. Spend time at the visitor center for a glance at copper headdresses, raven and toad effigy pipes, and a cache of five thousand shell beads. The orientation film provides some valuable information about the people who constructed the intricate earthworks that are found on the grounds.

  Outdoors, see the inside of a Hopewell burial site. Of special interest is the Mica Grave Mound. Part of this mound has been removed to expose the burial grounds of four individuals.

- Adena State Memorial, the restored estate of Thomas Worthington, Ohio's sixth governor and first U.S. senator, offers tours of the 1807 mansion. Limited hours of operation.

- Serpent Mound State Memorial, the largest snake effigy mound in North America, uncoils in the shape of a snake for almost a quarter mile. Who built this unusual formation? The mystery remains unsolved.

Tecumseh! The Outdoor Drama runs during the summer months only. For information on backstage tours and reservations, contact *Tecumseh!*, PO Box 73, Chillicothe, OH 45601; 740-775-0700 (March 1 through Labor Day weekend) or 740-775-4100 (all other times).

Other contacts: Hopewell Culture National Historical Park, 16062 State Route 104, Chillicothe, OH 45601; 740-774-1125. Adena State Memorial, Adena Road, PO Box 831, Chillicothe, OH 45601; 740-772-1500. Serpent Mound State Memorial, 3850 State Route 73, Peebles, OH 45660; 937-587-2796.

For area attractions, contact Ross-Chillicothe Convention and Visitors Bureau, PO Box 353, Chillicothe, OH 45601-0353; 800-413-4118 or 740-702-ROSS (702-7677).

Southeast

44

The Wilds

Twelve-year-old Ollie sauntered across the grass and nudged the rear corner of the parked bus. Thump! Ollie, a Bactrian camel, needed to scratch. Oblivious to the curious humans staring at her dark brown marble eyes, the two-hump camel rubbed her backside against the tour bus.

"Camels spit," cautioned our guide. "The odor from their stomach acid is ten times worse than a skunk's."

The windows remained shut.

We left Ollie and her family and continued our trek through "the Wilds," North America's largest endangered species preserve. In addition to camels, this area of the preserve, called the Asian pasture, houses African Cuvier's gazelles, Asian wild horses, and five-to-six-thousand-pound white rhinos. The rhinos living here participate in natural breeding programs as well as reproductive technology development.

In 1986, more than nine thousand acres of reclaimed surface-mined land was donated by the Ohio Power Company and American Electric Power to be used as a breeding center. The Wilds, snuggled deep in the Buckeye State's southeastern hills, provides a haven for rare and endangered species. A double fencing system encloses the animals in two open-range habitats. These fences protect the animals, keeping humans, dogs, and coyotes out of reach.

"What the Wilds provides for these animals are habitats very similar to their own and in which they will live most naturally. The animals are still confined to some extent, and the area is semi-artificial to them. However, this is better than a zoo," said Robert W. Reece, executive director.

The bus exited the vast Asian grasslands and then crept slowly along the unpaved road into territory called the African pasture. A herd of common eland, the largest of Africa's antelope and the only species not on the endangered list in the park, grazed within view. Eland, similar in size to dairy cows, make excellent surrogate mothers for some species.

"They can leap five to six feet in the air," said our guide.

We waited patiently for one to jump, but to no avail.

Just ahead on the gravel road, a foursome of deep brown-red female sable antelopes appeared. These ladies were obviously enjoying an afternoon snooze. Nearby, a glossy, chocolate brown male stood guard, making certain the harem was safe.

"Look to your right at the reticulated giraffes from southwestern Somalia and northern Kenya. They can reach heights of eighteen feet."

Were they awake or sleeping? We could only guess.

"Giraffes sometimes sleep standing up with their eyes half open," our guide informed us.

We continued our leisurely journey, keeping our eyes focused on the open range. Just ahead to our left side appeared several rare scimitar-horned oryx, and Hartmann's mountain zebras, the third most endangered of the zebra species.

As our mini safari began to wind down, we savored the last leg of our adventure, passing several lakes and ponds. These popular watering holes attract large gatherings of Canada geese and swans.

The bus returned its passengers to the visitor center. Some of us wandered around inside the gift shop. Others took a stroll outdoors and discovered an overlook. What a spectacular view of the pasture!

"In the Wilds, animals are living their lives among a variety of habitats—rolling grasslands, woodlands, spring-fed lakes, and ponds—and with a variety of other animals. Remember: you're in their space! If you take the time to watch, observe, and listen, you'll see how they live," advises Reece.

FOR MORE INFORMATION

The Wilds area is located south of Interstate 70 and west of Interstate 77 near the town of Cumberland. Hours of operation change with the season. Admission is charged for the one-hour bus tour. A snack bar and gift shop are available. For further information and detailed directions, contact the Wilds, 14000 International Road, Cumberland, OH 43732; 740-638-5030. Website: www.thewilds.org. Or contact an area visitors bureau: Zanesville–Muskingum County Convention & Visitors Bureau, 205 North Fifth Street, PO Box 3396, Zanesville, OH 43701; 800-743-2303 or 740-454-8687. Website: www.zanesville-ohio.com. Cambridge/Guernsey County Visitors and Convention Bureau, 2250 Southgate Parkway, PO Box 427, Cambridge, OH 43725-0427; 800-933-5480 or 740-432-2022. Website: www.cambridgeoh.com\guernseycountyinfo\.

The Wilds

45

Y-Bridge Country

ZANESVILLE

PLEASE—DON'T STRAIN YOUR NECK TRYING TO SEE WHAT Ripley's Believe It or Not describes as: "The only bridge in the world which you can cross and still be on the same side of the river." Just get off Interstate 70 at the Zanesville exit. Within minutes, a Y-shaped bridge will be in view. It stretches across the south-flowing Muskingum River, and also the Licking River that comes in from the west.

The history of the bridge dates back to 1814. The first Y-bridge, built of wood by city founder Ebenezer Zane, was carried off in a flood. It was immediately replaced by a covered bridge that lasted until the next flood. Y-bridge "number three" was wood and lasted sixty-eight years; the fourth bridge was made of concrete; the current bridge, made of concrete and steel, was opened in 1984. Best view of this one-of-a-kind structure? Head up to the Putnam Park Overlook, just off Pine Street.

Zanesville's popular bridge portrays only a piece of the city's heritage. "Clay City" and "Pottery Capital of the World" were nicknames in the past, and clay continues to contribute to the town's charm.

Perhaps "the girls" would love to indulge in a weekend shopping getaway. Fioriware, makers of hand-painted glassware, ceramic embossed dinnerware, and other coordinated accessories, operates a wonderful "seconds" store in the downtown's historic potter's alley. Then check out the pie plates, canisters, stoneware water kegs, and cookie jars at the Robinson-Ransbottom Pottery outlet shop. Located eight miles south of Zanesville, this factory is the largest stoneware plant in the world. Tours are offered.

Alpine Pottery carries a variety of hand-decorated stoneware made from local clays. Free factory tours are offered. Clay City Outlet Center, a huge freestanding log cabin, attracts year-round browsers. Discover a wide selection of pottery, housewares, and gift items.

The Freight Shops, former site of the New York Central Railroad depot on the corner of Market and Third Streets, comprise a small strip of stores that specialize in pottery, handcrafted items, year-round Christmas gifts, and locally made chocolates.

Need a break from the shopping scene? Then, stroll through the Zanesville Art Center and marvel at the impressive collection of modern, oriental, and European paintings. Be sure to view the extensive display of art pottery and the exhibits that feature sculptures, drawings, and graphics. Of particular interest on the first floor is the Panel Room. It was dismantled from a 1695 English manor and brought here to the art center. Walk inside the elegantly decorated room for a peek at originals by Turner, Rembrandt, and Rubens hanging from the walls.

More Stuff to Do

- Looking for another view of the Muskingum River? Book a cruise on the historic *Lorena Sternwheeler*. One-hour rides or two-hour dinner trips are offered from mid-May through mid-October.

- In 1810, Zanesville became the capital of Ohio for two years, before losing to the city of Columbus. The Stone Academy, in the city's historic Putnam district, was built to house the legislative seat. The legislature never met here, but two conventions of the State Abolition Society convened at this site in the 1800s. Take a self-guided tour of one of the earliest settlements in Ohio and see the Stone Academy, the 1825 Putnam Presbyterian Church, and several other 19th-century and early-20th-century structures.

- Plan a side trip to the National Road/Zane Grey Museum. Ask the gang to try to imagine a world without planes, trains, and automobiles. Travel would be *such* a chore. The museum, ten miles east of Zanesville, illustrates the story of pre-modern-day transportation. Wander throughout the rooms. You'll gain a real sense of travel on America's first federal highway.

  Find the 120-foot diorama, dotted with miniature figurines, primitive tools, and tiny pieces of wood. This intricate display portrays an excellent reproduction of the backbreaking story of the men and women who built the road connecting the East Coast with the western frontier. The diorama extends along an entire wall of the museum.

  As the years progressed, traffic became heavier and more congested. Livestock, Conestoga wagons, and stagecoaches caused deterioration of the road. Take note of the minute replicas of steam trains and motorcars in the exhibit. They are proof of a lessened need for a national road.

  Before departing the museum, check out the 1916 Model T Ford, located just outside of the Art Pottery room. Then wander into the Zane Grey Wing, dedicated to the author of adult western novels.

  Now—pile back in the car and be thankful for road progress!

Y-Bridge Country

- Canals are an integral part of Ohio's history. The Muskingum River Parkway features ten hand-turned locks between Marietta (south of Zanesville) and Dresden (north of Zanesville) that are still navigable by small craft. Even if you don't own a boat, a summertime afternoon drive along State Route 60, south of Zanesville to the Ohio River, provides spectacular roadside views of operating locks. The town of McConnellsville, just south of the Rokeby Lock, is home to an 1850s antebellum mansion. Travelers are invited to stop for a meal or take a stroll through the restored home, now the Howard House Restaurant.

- During the warm months, Muskingum County (including Zanesville) attracts outdoor enthusiasts. Area state parks offer camping, fishing, boating, hiking, and swimming.

For More Information

For information on all area attractions and events, contact the Zanesville–Muskingum County Convention & Visitors Bureau, 205 North Fifth Street, Zanesville, OH 43701; 800-743-2303 or 740-454-8687. Website: www.zanesville-ohio.com.

Other contacts: Zanesville Art Center, 620 Military Road, Zanesville, OH 43701; 740-452-0741. *Lorena Sternwheeler,* Zane's Landing Park, Zanesville, OH 43701; 800-246-6303. The National Road/Zane Grey Museum (located east of Zanesville), 8850 East Pike, U.S. Route 40, Norwich, OH 43767; 740-872-3143.

Boaters who wish to obtain a lock usage permit and visitors who are interested in the lock schedule should contact the Muskingum River Parkway State Park, PO Box 2607, Zanesville, OH 43702-2607; 740-674-4794.

Southwest

46

"Wright" Wings and More!

Weekend jaunts to Dayton often start at the United States Air Force Museum. However, some visitors bypass the city sights and head directly to Wright-Patterson.

"I've visited the museum probably a dozen times. There are so many things to see and so much written material, you can't cover everything in a day or two. I would say it's the nicest museum I've been too," said Rick Cytacki, a World War II buff, who makes the three-and-a-half hour trip from Michigan. "For a number of years it was our Good Friday field trip. My two sons and I would just stay the day."

Even visitors with a casual interest in flight are in awe of the "world's largest and oldest military aviation museum" located on the historic Wright Field portion of Wright-Patterson Air Force Base.

Self-guided tours begin with exhibits of people's fascination with flying machines, dating back to Greek mythology, and Leonardo da Vinci's 16th-century helicopter drawings. As you wander throughout the complex, look for the Wright brothers' artifacts: wind-tunnel scales, blueprints, an anemometer, and a Wright engine.

The rooms in the museum are mammoth. Look up at the rare ninety-two-foot-long World War I Caquot Type R observation balloon as it hovers above the crowd. It's believed to be the only one of its kind. Then check out the North American T-6G, an aircraft used for training fighter pilots during World War II. The cockpit of this plane is easily viewed from an attached platform.

Interested in prisoner-of-war belongings? Wire cutters, escape tools, and an oven made from tin cans fill one of many World War II display cases.

Take the kids by the hand and meander inside the Globemaster II (careful—it's dark!). "Old Shakey," as it was affectionately labeled in the early 1950s, could carry field guns, bulldozers, trucks, or two hundred soldiers.

Imagine the impact and destructive power of a two-hundred-pound supersonic air-to-air missile used in Operation Desert Storm. Visitors get a really close look at a collection of these missiles in the Modern Flight Hangar.

Be sure to experience the action of an IMAX film. Take a seat in the theater with the sixty-foot-high by eighty-foot-wide screen. Get ready for a powerful encounter that will draw you into the center of the action. The images on the curved screen appear so close, you'll want to touch them.

Before you leave the museum, wander into the bookstore. Once you've perused the shelves, perhaps you'll agree with our friend Rick, who describes it as "the best aviation bookstore I've ever seen."

FOR MORE INFORMATION

Admission is free to the United States Air Force Museum; however, there is a charge for the IMAX theater. For further information contact the United States Air Force Museum, 1100 Spaatz Street, Wright Patterson AFB, Dayton, OH 45433-7102; 937-255-3286.

47

The Queen City

CINCINNATI

IN OUR FAMILY, CINCINNATI PRESENTS AN OBVIOUS CHOICE
for a weekend ramble. Driving south on Interstate 75 from
Michigan, in the direction of the Ohio-Kentucky border, we
exit the freeway just shy of the Ohio River and head west.
Within minutes, the car is safely nestled in the parking lot at
Union Terminal, a historic train station with a striking
resemblance to an oversize, dome-shape radio. (The males in
my household possess a sixth sense when it comes to finding *anything* railroad related!)

Union Terminal overflows with delightful surprises aimed
at satisfying the casual traveler in search of an any-day-of-
the-week escape. Let's take a swing through the terminal
complex, and then we'll take a peek at some of the other
highlights of the Greater Cincinnati area.

Union Terminal

A magnificent rotunda decorated with murals signifying the
art deco era serves as the hub of the Museum Center at
Union Terminal. The mammoth complex covers the area of
fourteen football fields. Plan to spend at least a full day at the
center. You'll find the Cincinnati Museum of Natural His-

tory, The Cincinnati Historical Society Museum and Library, an Omnimax theater, an ice-cream parlor, museum shops, and food booths.

Turn right as you enter the station's concourse level for the Cincinnati Museum of Natural History. Inside the museum, take a walk through a glacier for a taste of life when one-ton ground sloths and saber-toothed cats roamed the earth. Your journey through a time capsule reveals tidbits about Cincinnati's reign as "Queen City of the West."

Before departing, check out the Children's Discover Center where kids learn, via hands-on activities, about the workings of the human body. Any preschoolers in the group? If there are, let them linger in the Dino Hall to play games and work on puzzles.

Return to the rotunda entrance and turn left into the Cincinnati Historical Society Museum. Here you'll find yourself following the footsteps of Cincinnati's legacy from its growth as a frontier river town to a modern urban society.

Wander inside the settler's cabin, board a pioneer flatboat, and climb into a ninety-four-foot side-wheel steamboat docked at a replicated 1850s Cincinnati Public Landing site. As you roam around the exhibits, costumed interpreters share tales of bygone days.

A library stocked with books, periodicals, maps, and newspapers dating back to the 1750s is free and open to the public.

From the concourse's entrance, the Omnimax Theater is a straight shot to the back of the terminal. The five-story domed screen offers the audience a hypersensory encounter. If you experience dizziness (lots of folks do!), just close your eyes for a few seconds.

When you've completed a sweep of the halls that thousands of World War II soldiers once passed through, make a final stop at the Rookwood Ice Cream Parlor (just outside the Museum of Natural History) and treat the gang to double-scoopers!

More Cincinnati Sites

- Do you know where all the sinfully delicious chocolate cakes and candy bars begin? (Not counting your mom's, grandma's, or best friend's kitchen!) Visit Krohn Conservatory, home of an impressive under-a-glass-dome rain forest, and search for a chocolate tree. This tree, native to Mexico and Central America, produces seeds and pods that are the source of all chocolate flavoring. If you're a chocoholic (like some of the neighborhood gang I know), you'll truly appreciate this bit of trivia.

  Elsewhere in the conservatory, discover a variety of papaya plants, orchids trimmed in soft hues, flamingo lilies, and a wonderful selection of exotic tropical flowers. The flower and plant arrangements are in sync with the changing seasons.

- On one side of the Cincinnati Art Museum are galleries lined with European impressionist and postimpressionist paintings. Across the hall, rooms are filled with American impressionist works. This setup allows art lovers the opportunity to compare the different styles.

  A recent renovation of this world-renowned museum highlights a collection of art that spans a period from ancient to modern times.

  On weekends, children, as well as adults, experience art via Family Fun Tours. The museum is free on Saturdays.

- You can't ignore the mighty Ohio River, Mother Nature's natural curve separating Cincinnati and Covington, Kentucky. Three bridges connect the two cities, providing easy access to several sight-seeing boat lines, which run excursions during the warm-weather months. For a panoramic view of the Cincinnati skyline, join a riverboat cruise from the Kentucky side of the river. (At present,

209

The Queen City

there are no riverboat cruises from the Cincinnati side; however, you can book cruises through the Greater Cincinnati Convention & Visitors Bureau.) Canoes, rowboats, houseboats, and yachts crowd the waters during the summer months.

A series of overlooks, grassy areas for picnics, sand volleyball courts, and an amphitheater add to the riverfront's popularity.

Take me out to the Cincinnati Reds ball game! Root, root, root for the home team! Each time the Reds, the first professional baseball team in the United States, hit a home run or win a game, fireworks explode over the stadium, creating a spectacular reflection on the river.

- Ohio's oldest and largest winery, Meier's Wine Cellars, features a year-round wine shop and tasting room. Tours are offered Monday through Saturday (by appointment only from November 1 to May 31).

- The only memorial to the country's twenty-seventh president is located in the Mount Auburn section of Cincinnati. The William Howard Taft National Historic Site, the restored home where Taft lived as a child and young adult, contains family portraits, original furniture, and books belonging to the Taft family. Admission is free.

- Federal architecture and early-19th-century furnishings highlight the intimate Taft Museum, the former home of the Charles Phelps Taft family (Charles was President Taft's brother). The cozy rooms include portraits by Rembrandt, Goya, and Sargent; Qing dynasty Chinese porcelains; and antique pocket watches. The museum is located five blocks from the center of downtown Cincinnati.

- Chili, anyone? You can't leave town without a taste of the local recipe. The Official Visitors Guide reads "Cincinnati chili is of Greek origin . . . served over spaghetti. A three-way begins with an oval plate of spaghetti, topped with chili and mounds of grated cheese. A four-way adds onions, and a five-way includes beans." Remember, order your chili either "three-way, four-way, or five-way." Try a plate. Do you detect a touch of cinnamon and chocolate, supposedly the two "secret" ingredients?

FOR MORE INFORMATION

For information on the area, contact the Greater Cincinnati Convention & Visitors Bureau, 300 West Sixth Street, Cincinnati, OH 45202; 800-CINCYUSA (246-2987). Website: www.cincyusa.com. For information on the Cincinnati Museum Center, the Cincinnati Museum of Natural History, The Cincinnati Historical Society Museum, and the Omnimax Theater, contact Union Terminal, 1301 Western Avenue, Cincinnati, OH 45203; 800-733-2077 or 513-287-7000.

Other contacts: Krohn Conservatory, Eden Park Drive, Cincinnati, OH 45202; 513-421-4086. Cincinnati Art Museum, Eden Park, Cincinnati, OH 45202; 513-721-5204. The Cincinnati Reds, 100 Cinergy Field, Cincinnati, OH 45202; 513-421-4510. Meier's Wine Cellars, 6955 Plainfield Pike, Cincinnati, OH 45236; 800-346-2941. William Howard Taft National Historic Site, 2038 Auburn Avenue, Cincinnati, OH 45219; 513-684-3262. Taft Museum, 316 Pike Street, Cincinnati, OH 45202; 513-241-0343.

For information on riverboat cruises and other Covington attractions, contact the Northern Kentucky Convention & Visitors Bureau, 605 Philadelphia Street, Covington, KY 41011; 800-447-8489.

The Queen City

48

Planes, Parks, and Packards

DAYTON

I HAD MY FIRST TASTE OF VIRTUAL REALITY IN A VIDEO ARCADE race car. Seated in the cars to my left were Jonathan, my son, and his two cousins, Vinny and Rob. The object of the game: first driver to finish the race wins. I lost control within the first eight seconds, veered head-on into a brick wall, flipped over three times, and crashed into my son's (or was it my nephew's?) vehicle. I finished last . . .

The Space Theater at The Boonshoft Museum of Discovery—Dayton, Ohio (formerly the Museum of Natural History) offers a similar optical-illusion adventure with a real special bonus. No losers—everyone wins!

"The theater is our most popular attraction," said Chuck Fields, information director.

"In addition to stars, we can do graphics. We recreate a model of the space system and fly you through it. We teach physics concepts via a visual illusion. It feels as though the room is moving as you fly through space. Visitors are taken on a voyage through a black hole."

Space gazers relax at the state-of-the-art planetarium show in comfy theater-like chairs. Fields advises: "If you feel dizzy, close your eyes, and the effect goes away. We assure people the chairs *are* bolted down—they are not moving!"

Once you're steady on your feet, check out the rest of the neat museum. You'll discover the Wild Ohio zoo, the home of furry, scaly, and feathery animals; a hands-on learning center with bones and antlers; and a light-and-laser science lab. Don't leave without participating in the hair-raising experiment.

More Dayton

- Carillon Park is a historical complex comfortably surrounded by acres of shade trees. The park focuses on the innovation, creativity, and dedication of the people who helped shape Dayton.

  Once you find the 1905 Wright Flyer III, note the differences between "the world's first practical airplane" and today's flying machines.

  Take a stroll through the well-groomed grounds. You'll discover a potpourri of exhibits: the Sun Oil Station (circa 1924); a two-man caboose; the Rubicon, a fireless locomotive; an 1800s covered bridge; and a replicated Wright Cycle Shop.

  On Sundays, listen to the serenade of fifty ringing bells from the carillon tower. The 151-foot-high landmark stands erect just before the entrance to the park.

- Searching for some trivia on the history of air travel? Then, spend an afternoon following the Dayton Aviation Heritage Trail, a National Historical Park comprising four sites. First, stop at the Wright Cycle Shop, a restored building used for the Wrights' businesses, and then wander over to the nearby Hoover Block, location of the Wright brothers' printing business.

  Next, visit the Dunbar House State Memorial, home of Paul Laurence Dunbar, the first African-American to write for white publishers. Dunbar was a friend and coworker of Wilbur and Orville.

The Huffman Prairie Flying Field, located at Wright-Patterson Air Force Base, provided the Wright brothers with a hangar and landing field. The Wright Flyer III, displayed at Carillon Park, completes the aviation tour.

- Perhaps Packards are more your style. If so, head downtown to the Citizens Motorcar Company: America's Packard Museum. Shiny vintage Packards blend in nicely with the art deco building at the intersection of Ludlow and Franklin Streets.

  The museum, originally a Packard distributorship from 1917 to 1940, is a delightful display of restored Packard automobiles, original articles of incorporation, an operational car elevator, and a working service department.

- Take a giant step back in time at SunWatch Indian Village, an archaeological park southwest of the city. The Fort Ancient, a prehistoric Indian group, lived here close to the Great Miami River. As modern visitors stand on the observation deck and gaze out at the oval-shape landscaped grounds, they immediately get a sense of 13th-century village life.

  Follow the self-guided walking trail. The quarter-mile loop is an easy stroll on mostly level land. Peek inside the reconstructed wood house built on the original location. Holes in the roof let smoke escape from the indoor fires.

  SunWatch, open year-round, hosts an array of demonstrations including flint knapping, arrow making, and tool making. Participate in a leather-working workshop; learn to use an awl, sinew, or other bone tools; or pretend to be a Fort Ancient farmer (reservations needed).

FOR MORE INFORMATION

For information on all area attractions, contact the Dayton/Montgomery County Convention & Visitors Bureau, 1 Chamber Plaza, Suite A, Dayton, OH 45402-2400; 800-221-8234 (in Ohio) or 800-221-8235 (outside Ohio). Website: www.daytoncvb.com.

Other contacts: The Boonshoft Museum of Discovery—Dayton, Ohio (formerly the Dayton Museum of Natural History), 2600 DeWeese Parkway, Dayton, OH 45414; 937-275-7431. Carillon Historical Park, 2001 South Patterson Boulevard, Dayton, OH 45402; 937-293-2841. Wright Cycle Shop/Hoover Block & National Park Service Office, 22 South Williams Street, Dayton, OH 45407; 937-225-7705. Paul Laurence Dunbar House State Memorial, 219 North Paul Laurence Dunbar Street, Dayton, OH 45401; 937-224-7061. Wright Flyer III/Wright Hall (see Carillon Historical Park above). Huffman Prairie Flying Field, 1101 Spaatz Street, Wright-Patterson AFB, Dayton OH 45433-7102; 937-257-5535, extension 254. Citizens Motorcar Company: America's Packard Museum, 420 South Ludlow Street, Dayton, OH 45402; 937-226-1917. SunWatch Indian Village, 2301 West River Road, Dayton, OH 45418-2815; 937-268-8199.

Southwest

49

Dickens Didn't Drink Here!

LEBANON

"We dine . . . and have nothing to drink but tea and coffee. As they are both very bad, and the water is worse, I ask for brandy; but it is a temperance hotel, and spirits were not to be had for love or money."

CHARLES DICKENS, ENGLISH NOVELIST, 1842; IN REFERENCE TO HIS STAY AT THE SIGN OF THE GOLDEN LAMB, LEBANON.

IF MR. DICKENS ORDERED A GLASS OF BRANDY TODAY AT THE Golden Lamb in Lebanon, the establishment would happily oblige. Temperance no longer exists.

The Golden Lamb, Ohio's oldest operating inn and restaurant, attracts modern-day travelers. They arrive thirsty, hungry, sleepy, or just plain curious. They leave satisfied.

Meals, served in one of several Early American–inspired dining rooms, are exceptional. Choose from a delectable changing menu: Milly Swidger's chicken leek pie, bronze braised beef with English ale, or braised oxtails. For the more traditional palate: entrees of roast pork loin on dressing, corned beef sandwiches, and chef's salad bowl are featured.

The historic guest rooms, named after literary and political figures who have slept in the hotel, lure overnight sojourners. Take a walk upstairs. Peek inside the unoccupied period-decorated rooms with door plaques titled "Charles Dickens," "John Quincy Adams," and "Wm. Henry Harrison."

Note the fine collection of Shaker artifacts scattered throughout the inn: a sewing desk, tailoring counter, sill cupboard, and two-slat chair.

Continue your stroll throughout the comfy quarters and try to imagine the inn's modest beginnings that date back to 1803. During that time period only about half of the population could read. A painted picture of a golden lamb, rather than a sign with words, was hung outside of Jonas Seaman's "house of public entertainment." An interesting, unofficial piece of folklore explains the reason why Jonas picked a lamb: The devil can assume any shape except that of a lamb.

When 19th-century stagecoach passengers arrived at the inn, they longed for Mrs. Seaman's home-cooked meals of wild turkey, hot corn bread, and apple butter. She served her guests at a common table. As the decades passed, the inn endured an array of colorful characters and activities: war sympathizers, ten U.S. presidents, authors, politicians, animal and circus acts, and live theater. Hospitality reigns at the sign of The Golden Lamb in the form of fabulous food and relaxed, circa-1800s accommodations. Reservations should be made well in advance.

The Warren County Historical Society Museum, one-half block south of The Golden Lamb, features an impressive collection of Shaker memorabilia, storefront exhibits surrounding a village green scene, horse-drawn vehicles, early farming tools, and folk art. Get a glimpse of the simple lifestyle of the Shaker religious sect, marvel at their meticulous wood-carved furniture, and learn the history behind their celibate beliefs. Shop for Shaker reproductions, decorative accessories, and books at the museum store.

All abooooard! The Turtle Creek Valley Railway engine chugs away from the Lebanon Station transporting train buffs on a twelve-mile round-trip excursion. Pulled by a diesel/electric locomotive built in the 1950s for the Chicago, Burlington and Quincy Railroad, the train rattles across the narrow-gauge tracks. Passengers press their noses to the windows for a view of the passing meadows and listen intently as crew members share stagecoach stories. Specialty excursions and discount days are offered.

The ovens at the Golden Turtle Chocolate Factory, across the street from the railroad station, tempt candy lovers. Try a taste (or bagful) of Texas Tortoises, pecan halves sinfully smothered in caramel and milk chocolate. Bet you can't eat just one!

Morrow

Drive southeast of Lebanon along the winding, two-lane State Route 123 to the town of Morrow, where fruit trees and horse farms dot the hillsides. Hidden behind a residential dwelling on Shawhan Road is The Workshops of David T. Smith, furniture builder. Park your car. Mild scents of freshly cut wood drift from the cabinet shop where cabinetmakers busily construct 18th- and 19th-century-style furniture. The simple, yet inviting, workshops beckon visitors to linger and learn. Watch the skilled crafters as they cut, carve, and finish reproductions of historical furniture.

Check out the pottery studio. Pay special attention to the potters' hands as they skillfully create lamp bases, jugs, and pots using Pennsylvania Dutch colors. The public is welcome to browse the villagelike grounds and showroom.

Next, continue your trek southeast from the Workshops until you reach the Valley Vineyards. Feeling hungry? Here you can choose your own steak, charcoal grill it, and sip some wine (there are fifteen varieties). The winery hosts a weekend Wine Festival in September.

Dickens Didn't Drink Here!

Kings Island

For family laughs, Paramount's Kings Island (approximately fifteen minutes from Lebanon) supplies a lengthy list of theme-park thrills: high-speed coaster action, a very messy game show called Mega Mess-a-Mania, the ultimate Days Of Thunder racing simulator, live theater shows, and fifteen acres of wet fun at WaterWorks. Here's the lowdown on the park from the "authorities."

"I liked the roller coasters. I went on one that goes upside down four times. It's awesome. There's a river ride I liked. It takes you by the waterfall and you get wet," said eleven-year-old Vinny.

Robert, nine years old, said: "Kings Island was really fun. It has water parks and lots of roller coasters. The one I like is the Vortex; I went on it twice. There's also the Beast. It's made out of wood, and it goes about sixty miles per hour!"

So, scream machines and water rides don't sound very appealing? Perhaps golf is more your style. Then, bring the clubs to the Golf Center at Kings Island, a public course designed by Jack Nicklaus.

Why Lebanon?

The town of Lebanon was named after the Middle Eastern country with the same name. Early settlers mistakenly believed the trees in their newly discovered land were cedar, similar to the trees growing near the Mediterranean.

FOR MORE INFORMATION

For further information contact The Golden Lamb, 27 South Broadway, Lebanon, OH 45036; 513-932-5065. Warren County Historical Society Museum, 105 South Broadway, Lebanon, OH 45036; 513-932-1817. Turtle Creek Valley Railway, 198 South Broadway, Lebanon, OH 45036; 513-398-

8584. The Workshops of David T. Smith, 3600 Shawhan Road, Morrow, OH 45152; 513-932-2472. Valley Vineyards Winery, 2276 East U.S. Routes 22 and 3, Morrow, OH 45152; 513-899-2485. Paramount's Kings Island, Interstate 71, exit 25, Kings Island Drive, Kings Island, OH 45034; 800-288-0808 or 513-754-5700. Open daily Memorial Day through Labor Day, and selected spring and fall weekends. The Golf Center at Kings Island, 6042 Fairway Drive, Mason, OH 45040; 513-398-7700 (for tee times) or 513-398-5200 (for office and restaurant).

For further information on Lebanon and surrounding communities, contact the Warren County Convention & Visitors Bureau, 1073 Oregonia Road, Suite A, PO Box 239, Lebanon, OH 45036; 800-791-4FUN (791-4386) or 513-695-1138. Website: www.ohio4fun.org.

Dickens Didn't Drink Here!

50

Miami County Stopover

Brukner Nature Center

NALA, A CREAMY BROWN BOBCAT, SITS ON HER PERCH. SHE
appears content in her cage. Her neighbor, a bald eagle
named Alexandria, and approximately thirty other animals
occupy the nearby cages at the Brukner Nature Center in
the town of Troy.

"We operate a wildlife rehabilitation center. We accept
any orphaned or injured native Ohio wildlife. Most of the
permanent animals on display can't survive in the wild," said
Debbie Brill, the Center's deputy director.

The staff believes that Nala was someone's pet because
she is declawed. Alexandria needed wing surgery after she
was hit by a car. Both animals are part of the year-round
outdoor exhibit near the Interpretive Building.

Brill explains what happens to the injured wildlife once
the Center receives them: "We have a vet on our staff. He
does the treatment. We fatten the animals up and then
release them. The rehab animals are not on display."

The displays in the Interpretive Building offer wonderful
close-ups of salamanders, snakes, foxes, turtles, and great
blue herons. A "touch" table lures kids. They get a chance to
finger an animal's skull and feel a snake's skin.

A nonscary Halloween program called Haunted Woods is
designed for preschool kids, their parents, and grandparents.

The group rambles through the woods in search of after-dark wildlife activity. Before the evening ends, everyone gets a chance to "talk" to the night forest.

Hiking is allowed all year long at Brukner, not just at Halloween.

"We have six miles of trails in diverse habitat. There is a fen (a type of wetland) area with a boardwalk, and a couple of ponds with turtles," said Brill.

The nature center, beautifully poised in the center of farm territory, extends for 165 acres. A bonus: admission is free Monday through Saturday. A small fee is charged on Sunday. Trails are always free.

More Miami County

- "One of the largest attractions in the county is the Piqua Historical Area State Memorial. It is a 175-acre historical farm site with one of the few authentic mule-drawn canal boat rides," said Diana Thompson, executive director of the Miami County Visitors & Convention Bureau.

  John Johnston, a U.S. Indian agent for western Ohio during the 1800s, lived on this farm. You can stroll the well-kept grounds in search of a two-story springhouse, a cider house, and Johnston's two-story mixed Dutch Colonial/Georgian-style farmhouse; listen to the costumed interpreters describe life in the 19th century; and watch craft demonstrations.

  Climb aboard! The *General Harrison*, a replica of a seventy-foot-long canal boat used for carrying people and goods in the mid-19th century, transports visitors on a restored section of the Miami and Erie Canal. The boat ride instills in its passengers a greater understanding of the short-lived canal era.

- Courthouses come in all sizes and shapes. If anyone should suggest that you take a look at the Miami County Courthouse, go for it!

   "The courthouse is unique. It is a magnificent building, built in 1888 for $400,000. That was very expensive for the time," said Thompson.

   The ornate windows, the hand-painted frescoes, and five domes designed after the U.S. Capitol in Washington combine to make an impressive county government headquarters.

   Thompson encourages travelers to just "wander in during the week, or make an appointment."

- The Miami County Park District operates fabulous stretches of land that offer the general public a wide range of year-round activities. Here's a look at some of the parks' facilities:

   A rushing waterfall at Charleston Falls Preserve is best seen from a boardwalk viewing area. Hiking trails and cross-country ski paths attract outdoor enthusiasts.

   The sixteen-hundred-foot boardwalk, near the river on the Stillwater Prairie Reserve, is constructed of recycled plastic planking. Hikers, bird-watchers, and cross-country skiers relish the vast fields and woodlands dotted with uncommon plants, soaring turkey vultures, and deer.

   Are you a fisherman (or woman)? For the rigorous soul, hip-boot wading is allowed in the river at Stillwater. Less strenuous-minded anglers fish in the man-made ponds.

   Garbry's Big Woods Reserve & Sanctuary overflows with exceptional animal and plant life. Step lightly across the "almost mile-long" boardwalk for views of an undisturbed wet beech-and-maple forest. Bring a picnic basket

Miami County Stopover

and your fishing poles in the summer months; dress warmly in the winter and try the cross-country ski trails.

- Outdoor art, sprinkled around the county, ranges from the abstract to the traditional to folk art. Each piece tells a story. Limestone, bronze, granite, aluminum, and stainless steel are some of the materials used. Time permitting, see all the art structures (there are nearly one hundred pieces) or pick and choose the ones you want to view. A detailed map of selected sculptures is available from the Miami County Visitors and Convention Bureau. Here's a brief look at two of the popular structures:

    Sound Chamber, a 20th-century interactive sculpture, sits in a park in the city of Troy. The geometrical design was inspired by the concept of musical ceremonial structures. Go ahead, step right up to the sculpture, and "play" it.

    Concrete molded over chicken wire was used for *Chester, the Blacksmith* located in Tipp City. The artist hid a time capsule inside Chester's body.

FOR MORE INFORMATION

For information on all Miami County attractions, contact the Miami County Visitors and Convention Bureau, 405 SW Public Square, Suite 272, Troy, OH 45373; 800-348-8993 or 937-339-1044. Website: www.tdn-net.com/miamivcb.
Other contacts: Brukner Nature Center, 5995 Horseshoe Bend Road, Troy, OH 45373; 937-698-6493. Piqua Historical Area State Memorial, 9845 North Hardin Road, Piqua, OH 45356; 800-752-2619 or 937-773-2522. Miami County Courthouse, 215 West Main Street, Troy, OH 45373; 937-332-6800. Miami County Park District, 2535 East Ross Road, Tipp City, OH 45371; 937-667-1086.

51

Swords, Shops, and Sauerkraut

WAYNESVILLE

Hear ye! Hear ye! Waynesville invites sojourners to its seasonal celebrations and year-round antiquing. Without further ado, let us begin our travels with a step back to the days of jousting, chivalry, and knights in shining armor.

Renaissance Festival

Willy-Nilly-on-the-Wash. Such a silly name for a village. Bizarrely dressed characters roam the streets shouting strange-sounding proclamations. Methinks a visit is in order.

Each year during the late summer and early fall, 16th-century England reigns at the Ohio Renaissance Festival. Little John meets Robin Hood for the first time; Stuart Sisk juggles heavy axes and swallows a flaming torch of fire; and comedic Celtic music swells from the pub.

Cheer for your favorite combatant as you watch a contest of staves and swords. Who will end up dripping wet?

Need some nourishment? Feast on giant turkey legs, steak-on-a-stake, hearty bread-bowl soups, and stews. Sip a soda, or sample one of the varieties of ales. Food and drink booths are plentiful.

Gather the gang together, and get ready for a costume change. How does Dad look in the garb of a noble? Who will wear the Maid Marian outfit? A photographer helps dress festivalgoers in period garments for a group photo.

Use paper and wax to create your own rubbing at a hands-on workshop. Not interested in producing your own keepsake? Then purchase a framed rubbing or print of historical significance.

Festival merchants demonstrate and sell their one-of-a-kind wares—a refreshing change from the mega-mall scene. The Metalmorphosis shop specializes in sun catchers, hanging dragons, knives, and masks. Select your favorite pair of earrings or a neckpiece at Uncommon Adornments. Jewelry is made from handcrafted semiprecious stones, beads, and bone.

Sit back, relax, and delight in the costumed performers as they bring pirates, peasants, and royalty to life. Catch a performance by Shakespeare himself; join the crowd at the pub and sing with the musical "triplets" ClanDestine; or get up and dance around the maypole.

At fifteen past the hour of three each day, Queen Elizabeth presides at the Children's Knighting Ceremony. Each child receives the title of Knight or Dame of the Realm. Certificates are issued by members of Her Majesty's court as a reminder of this special visit.

Stop at the petting zoo to see four-horned sheep, pygmy goats, and honking geese. Wonder if the mythical unicorn will make an appearance?

An actual wedding, wooing contests, games of strength and speed, and a harvest celebration by the villagers occur during theme weekends.

So, what are thee waiting for? Prepare thyself and partake! Methinks you'll enjoy this festival merriment.

Antiques

Can't make the Willy-Nilly scene at the Renaissance Festival? Not to worry. Just minutes west of the festival grounds is Waynesville, a town boasting to be the Antique Capital of the Midwest. The downtown shops, within a five-block area, attract serious antique dealers, casual savers, and the occasional treasure hunter.

Looking for a Christmas present for that hard-to-please sports-minded uncle? Surprise him with an antique putter or an old croquet set from the Golden Pomegranate Antique Mall. Brooches, pins, and necklaces reminiscent of Grandma's jewelry box are found at Stone Hinge.

Interested in teapots, Victorian furniture, brass lanterns, or dolls? You'll probably enjoy browsing any time of the year through the more than thirty-five shops and mini malls. Chances are you'll discover that hard-to-find trinket.

Sauerkraut Festival

During the second weekend in October, Waynesville celebrates "sour cabbage." Thousands of pounds of sauerkraut add a distinctive twist to traditional festival foods at the Ohio Sauerkraut Festival.

Now, don't turn your nose up just yet. First, sample the homemade brownies, chocolate fudge, bread, and cookies—all made with sauerkraut. Kids love pizza, right? Then, share a slice. Or try a doughnut, cream pie, or an old-fashioned sauerkraut dinner. When you've finished sampling the goodies, stay around and watch the entertainment. You'll also find booths filled with arts and crafts.

As your day draws to an end, surely you'll agree that King Cabbage makes a great excuse for a laid-back autumn afternoon.

FOR MORE INFORMATION

Rain or shine, the Renaissance Festival takes place five miles east of Waynesville in northeastern Warren County on State Route 73. The event is open weekends and Labor Day from late August through mid-October. For further information and festival dates, contact Ohio Renaissance Festival, Renaissance Park, PO Box 68, Harveysburg, OH 45032-0068; 513-897-7000.

For information on antiquing and the Ohio Sauerkraut Festival, contact the Waynesville Chamber of Commerce, PO Box 281, Waynesville, OH 45068; 513-897-8855.

For information on all area attractions, contact the Warren County Convention & Visitors Bureau, 1073 Oregonia Road, Suite A, Lebanon, OH 45036; 800-791-4FUN (791-4386) or 513-695-1138. Website: www.ohio4fun.org.

52

Yellow Springs Fever

CITY FOLKS FLOCKED TO YELLOW SPRINGS BY STAGECOACH during the 1800s. They headed for the town's spring waters in hopes of reaping therapeutic benefits. Modern visitors arrive here in search of a laid-back getaway and discover undertones of the 1960s era.

"The community is open-minded, with a focus on the inner self. There are spiritualists, tarot readers, and many New Age shops. Yellow Springs has a charming main street packed with neat shops where local artists sit and create," said Amy Weirick, Ohio's public relations manager, Division of Travel & Tourism.

Specialty stores in the hub of the compact downtown streets present an intriguing mix of nonmall wares. You'll find some unusual items, such as functional pottery, South American imports, handmade clothing, vintage fashions, and custom stained glass.

Following an afternoon of shopping, satisfy your hunger. Local eateries serve wonderful homemade meals, health foods, and gourmet coffees. At Carol's Kitchen, choose a sandwich and a bowl of soup (the potato is yummy). The heartier you eat, the more it costs—you pay by the pound. If you're in the mood for a glass of wine with your meal, mosey on over to the Winds Cafe. For that down-home-on-the-farm atmosphere while you eat, try the Golden Jersey Inn.

Neighboring Sites to See

- Drive a short jaunt northeast of Yellow Springs to Young's Jersey Dairy. (Same owners as the Golden Jersey Inn.)

  "Young's is a working dairy farm. They have a dairy operation that visitors can see. It is very family oriented. The food is outstanding. The ice cream is so fresh, you can taste the difference from cow to cone," says Weirick.

  Don't leave the farm without ordering a cone piled high with generous scoops of homemade peaches-and-cream or chocolate-fudge-brownie ice cream. The dairy serves at least thirty other flavors of ice cream late into the evening hours.

- Lumberjack pancakes are a really *big* deal at Clifton Mill in the village of Clifton, a long stone's throw east of Yellow Springs.

  "The pancakes are made from the flour the mill grinds," said Cheryl Bierley, support services coordinator for the Greene County Convention and Visitors Bureau.

  She recommends: "Get in line when the restaurant opens." During the breakfast and lunch hours, lines sometimes extend beyond the door.

  The historic, water-powered mill is the largest operating gristmill in the United States. Join the tour and watch the process of flour making. Or check out the collection of flour sacks—it's amazing to see what happened culturally as flour sacks changed.

- Reserve a seat beneath the summer stars on the outskirts of Xenia (say: ZEEN-ya), a comfortable ride just minutes south of Yellow Springs. Whiffs of gunpowder and dust from thundering horses' hooves trickle among the 1,200 viewers seated in the amphitheater. A three-acre stage, decorated with real props of stately trees and a winding creek, provides the backdrop. *Blue Jacket*, an epic outdoor drama, is the true story of a white man adopted by the Shawnee Indians. He eventually becomes their war chief.

Xenia is centrally located in the "transportation triangle," a reference to three major highways—Interstates 70, 71, and 75.

- The Greene County Historical Society in Xenia presents a nostalgic peek at the past. Visit the gracious and finely detailed rooms of the 1877 Queen Anne Victorian Town House; the Galloway Log House (circa 1799), one of the county's first homes, and site of frequent visits by Tecumseh, a Shawnee warrior; and the Carriage House Museum, home of an operating, detailed diorama with model trains and streetcars.

- Get outside! Acres of hiking and biking trails twist and bend throughout the rolling farmlands and villages of Greene County. Several state parks and nature preserves provide year-round activities for outdoor enthusiasts of all levels.

Bring your fishing poles and picnic baskets to John Bryan State Park (north of Xenia). Put on your hiking boots and follow the trails along the scenic Little Miami River gorge, climb the layers of bedrock, or reserve a campsite.

Crystal-clear waters and a 1,300-foot beach provide a swim-and-sun break, just south of Xenia at Caesar Creek State Park. A campground with several hundred shady and sunny sites, boat docks, and fishing for smallmouth and largemouth bass entice families. Hunting is permitted in the wooded lands, once the home of early-Ohio Native Americans.

The Little Miami State Park is loaded with historic sites: Indian mounds, relics, gristmills, and stagecoach

Yellow Springs Fever

trails. In the mood for canoeing? Follow the twisted Little Miami River—it renders more than eighty miles of canoeing possibilities. A trail corridor supplies a slew of family-style recreational opportunities—bicycling, hiking, cross-country skiing, in-line skating, backpacking, and horseback riding.

Clifton Gorge State Nature Preserve houses more than 460 species of plant life. Hike the colorful, steep, and sometimes slippery trail in the gorge. Or search for the remains of a brick stagecoach inn, check out the tumbling waterfalls, and absorb some pretty spectacular views of the preserve from the cliff's edge.

- Escaped slaves journeyed to the Underground Railroad station in Wilberforce during the 1800s. The town, located northeast of Xenia, has existed as an African-American settlement since that time. The National Afro-American Museum and Cultural Center, built on the original campus of Wilberforce University, presents one of the nation's largest collections of African-American artifacts.

- Meander around in the car throughout the county's back roads. Find five covered bridges constructed in the late 1800s through the early 20th century. A map of the two-hour loop is available from the Greene County Convention and Visitors Bureau.

- Looking for more shopping? The choices are endless. Browse Bellfair Country Stores and Restaurant, a seven-store complex specializing in crafts, gourmet foods, antiques, jewelry, and Christmas collectibles. Got an itch for the big mall scene? Nestled between the towns of Fairborn and Beavercreek is the Mall at Fairfield Commons, boasting five anchor stores, 150 specialty shops, and a food court.

FOR MORE INFORMATION

For information on all attractions, contact the Greene County Convention and Visitors Bureau, 1221 Meadowbridge Drive, Suite A, Beavercreek, OH 45434; 800-733-9109. Website: www.greenecountyohio.org.

For information on the outdoor drama contact the Blue Jacket Box Office, PO Box 312, Xenia, OH 45385; 937-376-4318.

State Park information: John Bryan State Park, 3790 State Route 370, Yellow Springs, OH 45387; 937-767-1274. Caesar Creek State Park and Little Miami State Park, 8570 East State Route 73, Waynesville, OH 45068-9719; 937-897-3055. Clifton Gorge State Nature Preserve, 3790 State Route 370, Yellow Springs, OH 45387; 937-964-8794.

Other contacts: Young's Jersey Dairy, 6880 Springfield-Xenia Road, Yellow Springs, OH 45387; 937-325-0629. Clifton Mill, 75 Water Street, Clifton, OH 45316; 937-767-5501. Greene County Historical Society, 74 West Church Street, Xenia, OH 45385; 937-372-4606. National Afro-American Museum and Cultural Center, 1350 Brushrow Road, PO Box 587, Wilberforce, OH 45384; 937-376-4944. Bellfair Country Stores and Restaurant, 1490 North Fairfield, Beavercreek, OH 45432; 937-426-3921. The Mall at Fairfield Commons, 2727 Fairfield Commons, Beavercreek, OH 45431; 937-427-4300.

235

Yellow Springs Fever

Index